The Forest Fire

What Can Happen When Students Pray

by

Dustin Hedrick

& Daniel Kim

Dustin Hedrick Publishing
PO Box 601
Emmitsburg, MD 21727

www.theforestfire.org & www.dustinhedrick.com

Ordering Information:
Quantity sales. Special discounts are available on quantity purchases by corporations, associations, and others. For details, contact the publisher at the address above.
Printed in the United States of America
Publisher's Cataloging-in-Publication data Hedrick, Dustin. The Forest Fire / Dustin Carl-Lee Smith Hedrick.
978-0-9903369-1-4
The main category of the book —Non-fiction —Religion.
First Edition

Facebook: http://bit.ly/facebook-forestfire
Twitter: http://bit.ly/twitter-forestfire
Our website is here: http://theforestfire.org/

THANK YOU

I first want to say thank you to a few people that have been huge in both this story and bringing this work to you today. Thank you, Daniel Kim for being a life long friend who has been there to do the crazy things with me and who not only goes out on a limb with you but will fall off and take on the next tree alongside you. You are an amazing friend and 2x2 partner in faith. Thank you to Ashely Shepherd for taking the time to read this book and edit it as well as for all of the other writing you have done for the last couple years to help me in ministry. You are amazing as well as thank you to Ryan, your husband and another one of my close brothers in the faith for sharing her with us. Thank you to Birchie Holliday for editing this thing on the final round. You are amazing at what you do. You brought this thing to life for us and thank you to Bill, your husband for sharing you with us as well as all the amazing valuable insight he has given me over the years. You two are awesome. Thank you to my mom, Vickie Hedrick for being the first to read everything I do as well as for making sure I keep it real. You help me stay honest! And thank you to my lovely wife, Lori for all the support and encouragement. I love you and would never have come this far without your tireless support!

Dustin

CONTENTS

DEDICATION

DUSTIN

I dedicate this book to the students that come after me. I intend only to leave a history and a legacy and I desire to see that you are encouraged. It may seem daunting, it has seemed that way before. However, GOD can do more than you can ever expect. If GOD can use a farm boy from the backside of North Carolina, then he can definitely use you.

I share this story and the things I have learned over many years of living and doing ministry in order to see that the next generation become all that GOD has called them to be. So, this book I leave and this story I share now for my kids and their kids as well as every one of you that would consider yourself mentored by me whether in person or through the writings. This is my gift to you. Now go and do something! I believe in you. GOD is behind you!

PREFACE

I want to preface this book with the following. First, this book is written from two people's perspectives. Although at times it did not seem like it, there were many others out there being stirred and used by GOD during this time of revival. Like Elijah, often we feel like we are the only ones that are following GOD when we are alienated and alone. And yet, GOD can have a remnant out there waiting to join in and accomplish something bigger than you could fathom. Often this remnant is feeling the same way we are and we will run into them divinely when it is time. So, if you were one of those folks like the guys with "Waymakers, NGM, IVCF, CCfC" and other groups we found later who were also seeking GOD at the same time for a revival work on campus and we just didn't cross paths until later, please do not hate this book. Contact us and share your story or better yet, add your story by writing about what happened with you on campus during the 1993-1997 season.

Second, we do NOT state at any point that we were mature or we made the best decisions. As a matter of fact, we were immature and learning from GOD each step of the way what HE would have us do and HE was maturing us in the process. So, if you knew us or know us now, I assure you, we do NOT have it all together. We do not. And actually, that is the gift of knowing GOD. HE often takes the "are-not's" and uses them dramatically because it shows off how great HE is. So, again, just because we were used does not automatically ascribe maturity to us during those years. Yes, we were passionate and set apart, however, there were folks I am sure that we hurt with our zeal. So, please forgive us and learn from what is good in this story and move forward today.

Third, we are encouraged that in our telling this story, it has already led to many of the next college and high school generations being stirred by GOD for something more. Some of you are already out there doing something. We are with you. We are committed to putting our resources, our experience and our finances behind you. We are committed to seeing you become a success. Our encouragement; let us know who you are. We want to support what you are doing. WE DO NOT WANT TO OWN IT. WE WANT TO EMPOWER YOU. There were very few that believed in us and what we were doing and we know what it is like to be out there taking risks and people thinking you are crazy. Do not be afraid to fail. Failure is awesome as long as it is a teacher. If failure educates us in how to do things better, then we are thankful for failure as well as success. DO NOT be afraid to look stupid and fail. Those that fail and shake it off become the best at success so long as their success doesn't own them. Do not allow success to own you. If you are a success at something, it is not who you are. Always find your identity in Christ and do NOT allow men's applause to move you. We bow for the applause of ONLY ONE!

So, fail fast, fail big and get it out of the way up front. Learn from failure. Read about the greats and repeat or experiment with what the great men and women of GOD did before you. As well, read about the great movements of GOD. And do not be moved by movements. Be moved by HIS SPIRIT ALONE! Learn to listen. Learn to obey simply. Press in. HAVE REVIVAL!

If you want more information about how to hear GOD and how to know Holy Spirit or more about revival in general, get my book, "The Warrior's Manual."

So, read through the story or skip to the end where you'll find steps on how to do this yourself on your campus. It is an experiment. Reach out to us and let us know who you are and what you are doing. When you do, we will do our best to provide you resources to see that you can connect with others like yourself at campuses throughout the world. And know this; we do not need somewhere to speak nor do we wish to get your money. We are only out to share a story and leave a legacy for Christ!

And as the game goes on, tag you're it!

-Dustin

FORWARD

It needs to be noted, the time in which we speak of was in years past and in some ways in the larger culture, things have changed drastically such as in technology. During that timeframe, email was something that had a lot of numbers and letters and an "@" sign. It was all text based, when now, you can have your own name in the email. And back then, the web was new and not image based. I actually got to build one of the first image based websites (it was such a novelty, almost every image we used could move). Our idea of a cell phone was a huge thing with a pull up antennae that you had to carry in a bag or in your car. We relied on using pagers for communication. We were creative with codes and such for prayer. It was awesome.

Now, the digital age is upon us and everything is moving at the speed of light. However, one thing has not changed. The life of students were riddled with challenges we still face today, including whether or not to stay chaste for their wedding day (few of my friends chose that route, therefore I was seen as weird). There were many that chose to do drugs and escape from the world around us rather than attempt to change it. People were as they are now, interested in creature comforts and because of this, it was hard for me to be a senior in high school that desired to see GOD shared through our drama team, outreach ministries, missions or even at rallies at schools or "See You at the Pole" events (which by the way, is the first time I ever preached the Gospel outdoors).

I was not perfect. I had my share of challenges. I wanted to be cool so I tried out curse words. The time I tried them out, my youth pastor caught me. Thank GOD he called me out on it. I even tried illicit substances like alcohol as a teen. I just didn't fit in that world so it didn't stick. I was always drawn to something more.

There may be new drugs. Peer pressure may begin at a younger age.

There have been many advances made to explicitly share all the forms of nudity that are now readily and easily available. Though available through different vehicles, the temptations are the same. The demonic spirits behind them are still the same. The flesh is still the same. The battle is still the same.

And with that said, I do not believe that this generation nor any other generation before it has a "sin" problem. I believe they have a VISION problem. Proverbs 29:18 says that without "vision," or in the Hebrew, "Prophetic Revelation," the people perish or again in the Hebrew, "They cast off restraint."

Does it feel like we live in a time where people have cast off restraint? Does it feel like people are "perishing" around us? It is NOT a problem with the sin. The sin is a symptom of another disease. The disease is "DE-VISION." It is a breaking down of vision. It is a killing of dreams and vision and a stopping of GOD's ability to prophetically reveal our purpose on the planet. Our purpose is wrapped up inside of HIM and HIS love and we have lost that love. However, if that love were again revealed, we would be awakened to it and radically changed forever.

When a middle school kid goes to school looking unkempt it makes his mother angry at the way he lives. If his mother yells at him for this, it will not cause him to change. However, if some cute girl winks at him or sends him a love note, that kid will head home, shower, cleanup his room, get clean clothes and go back to school dressed to impress.

What changed his life? Was it the fact his mom kept yelling? NO!!!! IT was the fact that he got a vision. He got a vision of LOVE! Once he was changed by love, he wasn't able to go back. Love had been awakened and no amount of "yuck" could hold him back.

Once we have a vision of love and JESUS' love has been revealed to us, we will be ruined for anything else in this world. Then, that revelation will open our eyes to our need for cleanup. The problem is a vision problem. The problem is a revelation problem. The problem is a LOVE REVELATION problem.

May this story wake you up to GOD. May your eyes be opened to HIS LOVE. May you believe you can be used and that HE can move again. May the gift of a changed heart and a turning from our sin story come again. May the joy of the cleanup of leaving our ways and joining HIS way return.

Pray with me here:

GOD, open my eyes. Help me to see YOUR LOVE revealed. Awaken me to YOUR desire for me and who YOU are and who I am in YOU. Show me YOUR plan. Give me vision. Give me the gift of repentance. Stir me up so that even the tough things YOU may show me feel good in the light of YOUR being my father and I YOUR child. May I never be the same. Help me to believe that YOU can do anything. Amen.

1 WHY WE NEED GOD'S MANIFEST PRESENCE

WHAT IT IS:

Let's start with understanding what Manifest Presence is. First, know this, there have been seasons in history that I describe as waves of GOD's movements. We have had moments that we consider high water marks in our lives where GOD has moved in such a way that it was more tangible than at other times. During these periods, we were hungry for GOD, desperate for more of HIM. There was a heightened sensitivity to HIS nearness as well as a desire for doing the life of Jesus and reading HIS word. At times, reading HIS word was like eating or drinking and we were totally into the verse, "As a deer pants for water, so my soul longs for YOU…"

We often experienced this with a group of believers in a church, campus ministry, or small group. The crest of these experiences was our desire to tell everyone else about what GOD was doing. There was an elevated concern for people knowing Jesus personally. There was also a drive to share with people outside our own small groups what GOD was doing. This kind of excitement led us to do some pretty crazy things, from our wearing clothes to our getting a tattoo or something else that demonstrated our love for Jesus and the love HE was stirring between us and others.

Having led youth ministries for many years to my 20 years of pastoring, church planting and missions, I have seen young people have this experience at a summer camps or retreats and I have seen it spill over from those events into the churches they attended as well as their homes, schools and communities. Now, the jaded, high church talking, walking dead in our congregations that I called, "The Frozen Chosen," would often comment, "Ah, they are just excited. It will wear off." And due to the lack of support and the literal push back from the older crowd as well as the lack of support from parents who did not like having to drive their kid to a gas station before church so they could share about Jesus with an attendant would kill this fire in these young hearts.

I believe this was something that was NOT supposed to wear off. GOD had come near.

This is a place we can live for the long haul. We just have to fight all the "fire extinguishers" in our lives and surround ourselves with the right stuff. But, before we talk about those things, if you have had any of these experiences, do NOT look down on them. REMEMBER THEM. Press in right now and pray before going on, "Father, in Jesus' name, remind me of how I have loved YOU more and when YOU were my first love. BRING ME BACK to that place of intimacy and passion and awaken my soul to long for YOU, to become desperate, not unthankful, and in a way that fights complacency. Reveal where I am overfed and unconcerned. Forgive me. I am sorry for becoming hardened. Soften my heart to feel YOU again and YOUR desire for my community and me. Draw me back to you..."

I believe that we're never supposed to simply live from high points in the faith alone. We were supposed to go from these mountaintops back to the valleys, refilled for the good and the bad in the journey, always finding our capacity from HIS proximity in our lives. We should have been encouraged to go deeper rather than wait for the high to wear off. We should have made prayer closets and spent time in worship. We can still change this. It is true that GOD moves in waves such as the sea and it is true that after every wave there is an undertow or pullback, however, it is not for the crests of the wave we live. We live in both the valley and mountain top, we live in both the crest of the wave as well as the trough. We know that the undertow of the pullback often causes the next crest of the wave. Learning GOD's characteristics at the height of each wave or the low of the troughs is crucial. Over time as the crests, troughs and undertows continue, we finally get to see the tide come in. We learn to wait in hopeful anticipation for the day that this tide comes in.

Awakening, revival and Manifest Presence are that "tide" coming in. Just because we are currently in a trough does not mean our GOD is not big enough to bring on another wave and not just another wave, but the tide. I believe there will be a tidal return when the Bride of Christ is in her glory and revealed. I believe there are tides at each of the historical awakenings, many of which were just after a trough (See historical records of lack of chastity of women in the colonies as well as British rule before 1740). Don't forget, GOD was silent for 400 years after Malachi lived till Jesus was born. It is not abnormal for GOD to bust out a killer wave after being silent. HE doesn't see that as a bad thing. HE calls it the "fullness of time." And HIS time is not based on the hourglass. It is based on HIS activity (see the Greek behind chromos and kairos in the story of the man beside the pool of Bethsaida and Jesus).

So, just because it seems dark and all too quiet doesn't mean GOD cannot move again. I believe HE plans these things. HE knows that the loudest testimony will be heard when everything is quiet. HE knows that the smallest light's effect will be in perfect darkness. We are those little lights! We pray for the waves. GOD is so big that HE can out of nowhere bring a tsunami! We believe for the tide.

Bring on the tide, LORD!

WHAT IT DOES:

The Manifest Presence of GOD in Biblical record can be fully defined in Isaiah 61, which Jesus quoted in Luke 4. So, the characteristics of what takes place when the fullness of GOD comes both in the future and right now are:

Isaiah 61 Characteristics:
The Poor get good news.
The Brokenhearted are healed and hearts are bound.
The Captives hear the message of freedom and receive it.
Prisoners of darkness are released.
The year of the LORD's favor is proclaimed.
GOD's vengeance, which is, justice is proclaimed.
Mourners are comforted.
There is Provision for grievers in Jerusalem.
Everyone's Ashes are replaced with crown of beauty.
People have their mourning replaced with oil of joy.
Everyone's Despair is replaced with praise garments.
Those that are broken become the Oaks of righteousness for GOD's splendor.
The Ancient ruins rebuilt by those Oaks.
Devastated places are restored.
Ruined cities are renewed that have been devastated for generations.
GOD will be the focus of ministry and not man.
Those that believe will have the inheritance of all nation's wealth.

When these things are demonstrated, we can say as Jesus said, "The Kingdom has come upon you…" Or, we can say that the Kingdom of GOD is fully manifesting itself which in turn is said to be, "The Manifest Presence of GOD or GOD's Kingdom…"

Some further demonstrations of the Manifest Presence of GOD in the Bible are:

Daniel 8:17; 7-10, 15-19 - Daniel fell, had no strength, and was terrified by God's Presence

1 Kings 8:10,11 - The priest couldn't stand because of God's glory

2 Chronicles 7:1-3 - Solomon and priest couldn't stand because of God's glory

Acts 10:10, 21:1 - Peter and Paul fell into trances and see and hear into the spirit world.

1 Samuel 19:18-24 - King Saul and his antagonistic men were overcome by the Holy Spirit and prophesied as they neared the camp of the prophets.

Exodus 19:16 - Thunder, smoke, shaking of the ground, sounds of trumpets and voices were upon Mt. Sinai.

Exodus 34:30 - Moses' face supernaturally shines -Also, the cloud appeared by day and fire appeared by night with the Israelites in the desert.

Matthew. 17:2-8 - Jesus and his garment supernaturally made brilliant, supernatural cloud and visitation of Moses and Elijah.

Exodus 3:2 - Bush was burning but not consumed.

John 1:32 - The Holy Spirit descended in bodily form as a dove.

Leviticus 9:24; 1 Kings 18:38; 1 Chronicles 21:26 - Fire from heaven consumed the sacrifices.

2 Corinthians 5:12, 13 - Paul described being "beside himself" as opposed to being "sober."

Luke 2:35 - A virgin conceived the Son of God.

John 18:6 - Unbelieving guards thrown to the ground.

Acts 9:4 - Saul of Tarsus saw brilliant light, was thrown from his horse, heard Jesus audibly, and was temporarily struck blind.

Revelation 1:17 - John fell as dead, had no bodily strength, and saw and heard into the spirit world.

HISTORICAL PRECIDENCE FOR THE MANIFEST PRESENCE OF GOD

Further in history there are many more, I am adding a few.

CHARLES FINNEY

Charles Finney tells of times when he would enter into towns and the heaviness of GOD's Presence would come upon the entire city. In this story, the Presence of GOD came on Antwerp, NY

I had not spoken to them in this strain of direct application, I should think more than a quarter of an hour, when all at once and awful solemnity seemed to settle down upon them; and a some thing flashed over the congregation – a kind of shimmering – as if there was some agitation in the atmosphere itself.

The congregation began to fall from their seats; and they fell in every direction, and cried for mercy. If I had had a sword in each hand I could not have cut them off their seats as fast as they fell. Indeed nearly the whole congregation were either on their knees or prostrate, I should think, in less than two minutes from this first shock that fell upon them. Every one prayed for himself who was able to speak at all. I, of course was obliged to stop preaching, for they no longer paid any attention.

SECOND GREAT AWAKENING

I am adding one from the Second Great Awakening, at the Cane Ridge Revivals.

The following was the report of an atheist "free thinker" named James B. Finley, who attended the Cane Ridge, Kentucky revival in 1801: "The noise was like the roar of Niagara. The vast sea of human beings seemed to be agitated as if by a storm... Some of the people were singing, others praying, some crying for mercy in the most piteous accents, while others were shouting vociferously. While witnessing these scenes, a peculiarly-strange sensation, such as I had never felt before, came over me. My heart beat tumultuously, my knees trembled, my lip quivered, and I felt as though I must fall to the ground. A strange supernatural power seemed to pervade the entire mass of mind there collected...At one time I saw at least five hundred, swept down in a moment as if a battery of a thousand guns had been opened upon them, and then immediately followed shrieks and shouts that rent the very heavens...I fled for the woods a second time, and wished I had stayed at home." (Quoted from When the Spirit Comes With Power by John White p.70)

WELSH REVIVAL (R. B. Jones journals)

A sense of the Lord's presence was everywhere. It pervaded, nay, it created the spiritual atmosphere. It mattered not where one went the consciousness of the reality and nearness of God followed. Felt, of course, in the Revival gatherings, it was by no means confined to them; it was also felt in the homes, on the streets, in the mines and factories, in the schools, yea, and even in the theatres and drinking-saloons. The strange result was that wherever people gathered became a place of awe, and places of amusement and carousal were practically emptied. Many were the instances of men entering public-houses, ordering drinks, and then turning on their heels leaving them on the counters untouched. The sense of the Lord's presence was such as practically to paralyse the arm that would raise the cup to the lips. Football teams and the like were disbanded; their members finding greater joy in testimony to the Lord's grace than in games. The pit-bottoms and galleries became places of praise and prayer, where the miners gathered to worship ere they dispersed to their several stalls. Even the children of the Day-schools came under the spell of God. Stories could be told of how they would gather in any place they could, where they would sing and pray in most impressive fashion. A very pretty story is that of a child of about four in an infant class who held up his hand to call the teacher's attention. "Well, A—," inquired the teacher, "what is it?" Swift and telling came the words, "Please, teacher, do you love Jesus?" That was all: nay, it was not all; the arrow had reached its mark. There and then the teacher came to the Lord, and it is only a year or so since death ended her great missionary career in India.

This all-pervading sense of the presence of God even among the children, may perhaps be further illustrated by a story from Rhos. Someone overheard one little child ask another, "Do you know what has happened at Rhos?" "No, I don't, except that Sunday comes every day now." "Don't you know?" "No, I don't." "Why, Jesus Christ has come to live in Rhos now!"

D.L MOODY

While in New York on business, the Holy Spirit's power fell. Here is how Moody described it. "One day, in the city of New York — oh, what a day! — I cannot describe it, I seldom refer to it; it is almost too sacred an experience to name. Paul had an experience of which he never spoke for 14 years. I can only say that God revealed himself to me, and I had such an experience of His love that I had to ask Him to stay His hand." Moody was sure that if God did not lift His hand, he would die.

These are just a few stories of GOD's Presence. There are so many more throughout history. I only am able to share these for now. You search for more!

WHAT IT MEANS FOR US NOW:

Based on our ability to trail GOD's movement all the way from the beginning of Biblical times to now, it can easily be said that GOD has not stopped moving nor does HE intend to. This is NOT just a onetime deal. This is normal Christianity and we are living in an abnormal era where we can see GOD can do it again and we can easily discern that HE desires to do it again even now. We must pray like the prophet, "LORD, we have heard of your great deeds, we are in awe of YOUR fame, renew them in our day and in our time. Make YOURSELF known. In wrath, remember mercy."

I dare you to pray that verse now!

WHAT WE CAN DO TO PREPARE:

First, please forgive us the church for holding you up and killing your fire. Don't stop when they say stop anymore. GOD is looking for a generation that will rise up and take hold of HIM. HE is looking for a generation of broken, disenfranchised and "has been's" to allow HIM full control, to answer HIS invitation. HE said in the Bible that the violent will take the Kingdom by force.

So, do it. Take it. Have it. If the church has ticked you off, do NOT blame what GOD has designed, and do not stop chasing after HIM just because someone who has an official role or a title in the church has hurt you. STOP ASSUMING THEY ARE GOD. They may not even know HIM. The established church is NOT the church. The church is the entire crowd of living believers both here and now and those who have already gone before, who are alive in Christ. They are the ones that KNOW JESUS and HE KNOWS THEM BACK.

Therefore, if anyone does not have the fruit of the Spirit, which is love, joy, peace, patience, gentleness, kindness, goodness, faithfulness and self-control and they are only relating to you from a titled position in the church, DO NOT allow their words to hurt you or kill your momentum. FIGHT BACK!

Push back the push back! Take the Kingdom by force. Take it back from the institutions. Take it back from the titled ones. Take it back from the "position holders." Take it back! Take the Bible back from those who misuse it. Take the theology back from those that are not practitioners but instead dead theologians. Take the Spirit back from the wacky abusers. Take the Kingdom of GOD back. Take it by force. Not in violence by man's definition, but a violent, passionate, furious table flipping love for Jesus kind of way. The zeal for HIS Presence and Person comes from a life lived from a place of outflow of worship and love received through forgiveness like a foot washing, weeping, once sinner.

TAKE IT BACK! Worship for real. Pray for real. Seek for real. Get others to join you. DO NOT LET the ones that do not truly love GOD usurp the Kingdom. GOD is sick and tired of being locked in glass houses. HE WANTS TO LIVE IN OUR HEARTS AGAIN!

DO NOT LET ANYONE STOP YOUR FIRE!

Make a plan to keep your fire once it is started.

1 - Surround yourself with other passionate Jesus people.

2 – Fight to take every thought captive from the enemy.

3 – Get deep in the actual Bible. Don't let someone regurgitate it to you through sermons or even this book. Although they can be good, read and learn to hear Holy Spirit for yourself.

4 – Get to know Holy Spirit.

5 – Journal and pray specifically, pray for specific people to know Jesus and specific metrics you wish to see GOD do in your day.

6 – Dream BIGGER! HE is able to do exceedingly, abundantly, above all we can ask or imagine… So, make time and dream bigger. Ask bigger. Stop asking for things just inside of human ability. If you ask for human

sized things, you will get human sized results. If you ask for GOD-sized things, you will get what kind of results? GRRRR!

7 – Make a place or space that you deem holy and set apart for GOD. I had a closet. You can do whatever. Some of my friends had closets as well even though it was under their clothes which were hanging. It doesn't matter. Make it special and set aside time to be with HIM.

WATCH THIS VIDEO ON HAVING A PRAYER CLOSET

WATCH THIS VIDEO ON KEEPING YOUR FIRE

Lastly, get my book, "The Warrior's Manual" if you want to learn more about these habits and go even deeper. It can help. But more importantly, GO TO OUR WEBSITE TO JOIN THE MOVEMENT: www.TheForestFire.org

Here we go. I cannot wait to read the stories that come from your life as you attempt the divine experiment. I know you are going to do great things for GOD. Remember, the definition of "great things" is NOT to be defined by man. The guy that led Bill Graham to Jesus would be considered average by man's standards. He was led to Jesus by a guy who didn't do anything that great that we know of except serve at a church. And no, he wasn't the preacher, he just served. But one day he happened to lead Mordacai Hamm to Jesus and Hamm eventually led Billy to Jesus at a men's meeting.

What kind of legacy will you leave? I believe in you. This book is proof of that. This book is not doing its job unless a generation wakes up. It is written for you. Please do not reject it. It is a gift. I hope you will accept it and own it. It is yours. Just as the gift HE gave me of living out the stories you'll soon read.

2 THE FOREST FIRE STORY
DUSTIN HITS CAMPUS
FALL 1993

Dustin Hedrick: All right, before we get started, for the rest of this book, when we refer to "UNC," "Carolina" or "UNC Chapel Hill," we are referring to the University of North Carolina at Chapel Hill, better known as "The Tarheels."

So we're going to record the story of the UNC Forest Fire Event and the events leading up to the weekend and all that good stuff that happened around it. In 1993 I graduated high school and headed to UNC Chapel Hill. I remember getting there and within the first couple of days I realized there was not a strong group of believers that had set themselves apart wholly for GOD and HIS ways. I felt very alone.

DUSTIN SHARES THOSE FIRST MOMENTS FROM HINTON JAMES HERE

One of my friend's mom, from my old youth group used to really watch out for me during this time. She would call and check in on me to make sure I didn't lose my fire from high school. Not only that, she actually paid for a subscription to a Christian magazine and had it delivered to my dorm room so I would be encouraged. I got my very first one within a few weeks of my being there. All I had was a magazine and a passion for GOD.

You see, I was supposed to try out for the men's soccer team but I ripped my quadriceps in my right leg playing soccer and kicking football. There was no way to fix it so they said I would have to sit it out on the bench. I went from being recruited and invited to either play soccer or kick football for a couple of different schools to not being able to play at all.

To make matters worse, within the first week of being on campus, I caught the flu and was stuck in bed except when I mustered up enough strength to crawl out and go to class. I was stuck. I had lost myself, my future, my plans and my hope. I only had GOD.

This was on the cusp of my coming to the end of myself while traveling the summer prior in Scotland and seeing how big HE is and how small I am. I told GOD take all of me, I give up. I quit all my plans, I just wanted HIM. (At this point, I think every student should travel outside the USA and see how large the world is and do a mission trip if possible. It will change your view on life and the way you approach college. I did both).

So, I had been really torn from my comfort zone of attending a great youth group, a great church, and being known as the guy who lettered in 5 sports while high-fiving all the way down hallways on Monday morning after kicking field goals on Friday night. …To nothing…

…Just GOD and aloneness. But with GOD, you are never alone and HE was just doing whatever it took to draw me near HIS side. Stripping away all the stuff and showing me who HE designed me to be in HIM.

I found out I had a couple friends on campus from my old area and school, but it did nothing to change the fact that I had left comfort behind. I decided that if I had to rip off this Band-Aid, I had to do something worthwhile. It wasn't worth it if something did not change in Carolina. Deep inside of me a strange thing happened, I believed for the unbelievable as GOD began to reposition my desperate heart for HIS plan. HE was already at work and I was getting ready to join HIM. This was going to be fun and there were others that I had not met yet that were feeling the same way.

IN THIS CLIP FROM MAIN CAMPUS DUSTIN DISCUSSES HIS FEELINGS ON THE STATE OF THE UNIVERSITY IN 1993

CAMPUS "FAITH" LIFE

This is really important because it sets the stage for the life of the campus. Those who considered themselves believers were often timid and shy. Their spiritual nature was not deep at all. More often than not they lived double lives, with one foot placed in the faith life and the other the party life and all that entails, the parties, the drinking and the drugs. It was not different from any campus anywhere. The campus was not in very good shape at all. As a matter of fact, the year before, the school had won the Men's Basketball NCAA National Championship and had been rated one of the nation's biggest "party schools." In other words, it was known for NOT being like Jesus.

It needs to be said upfront, there were maybe a hundred people diligently seeking GOD at the University that we knew of, maybe even less. Back then, Campus Crusade for Christ wasn't what it is today. It consisted of 100 to 150 people tops, it just wasn't that well established. All of the other campus ministries available were fractured into about 42 little groups. Everyone was doing their best, but it just wasn't being moved and stirred by a manifesting of GOD's Presence with an outflow of passion and salvations. All of these campus ministries were actually small groups of 100 people or less. I believe the largest group at the time was InterVarsity. Even still, they were not doing well. None of them were. There was a real air of division between the groups as they tried and tried to grow their specific brand of Christianity on campus. Which was fine, it just wasn't GOD's best. There were some precious people involved but understand, it wasn't t like there were just amazing movements of GOD to join in on when we were first arrived on campus. It was dry. And largely, people were congregating, not being stirred and passionate followers of JESUS. It was no different than joining any other club. People were often just looking for a place to hang out in hopes of finding someone nice with similar backgrounds and experiences as them to date.

As a matter of fact, the Christian community was very small in 1993 and '94. If you do the math, there were around 30,000 students on campus while we were there; of those students, it's likely that there were less than 2000-3000 involved at any given time with the 42 campus ministries available.

I remember back in 1993 during the first few weeks of my arriving on campus just sitting in my room praying. I would just sit and pray and pray and pray everyday. Though I had no one else to join in with me and I felt so alone, I remained true to my habit of praying, fasting and seeking God.

HINTON JAMES, A QUICK LOOK AT THAT FIRST VIEW

Even before I left home to head to Carolina, I thought to myself, I am purposed to go there to see revival. That's something I guess you could say the Lord placed on my heart that summer during missions. I had already started praying, "God bring revival to this campus." I remember praying my first day, "Lord, even if there's not another believer here that's sold out to you and if everyone else is just "doing" church and then partying it up and doing their own thing the next day, send me, use me."

I didn't have a clear understanding of what revival and awakening looked like at this point in my life. I just knew I had been stirred during high-school when my youth pastor at the church I grew up in, "Tim" took me through one of the first editions of "Experiencing GOD" by Henry Blackaby. It was then than I started to understand what it meant to see GOD move in bigger ways than what we had currently called "normal" in the church.

Here and now in the 20th century in which we live, I'd have to say, the church is not passionate about GOD and is largely powerless. This may be what we are used to in our culture in America and it may be the "norm" but just like Americans are known to be "normal neurotics," which means that they are known to be normally abnormal, the church is now normally abnormal. We exist in a state of dysfunction. We are out of relationship with GOD and HIS Holy Spirit. We do not know how to hear HIS voice and do the will of GOD. There are no Kingdom fruit and gifts functioning and if there are, we grandstand them as if they are something weird and abnormal when they are the norm that Jesus called us to operate in all the time. When we grandstand the gifts they are mere "works" in HIS eyes, simple service to the world around us. In doing this, we shield others from being able to see the love of Jesus. In all that we do, we are commanded to do it in HIS name. Whether what we do is as small as giving someone a cold cup of water to drink, it should glorify HIM. It is HIM who rewards us. This defies the norm; we are NOT called to be normal. We have gotten used to something that is a historical abnormality. A church that is ritual, not relationship, that is powerless not powerful and that is consumer driven, not sacrificially servant-hearted.

So, back then as I read the stories Blackaby wrote about the great men and women of history as well as the great movements of GOD through history, I became stirred for something more. The "norm" I am no longer content with today is the same "norm" I experienced back then. It just wouldn't satisfy. All the while, as I was reading this book and being stirred was about the same time I became involved in dramas with our youth group from South River Baptist church. It is with this drama team that I traveled and went on missions. We saw many people come to Jesus and accept Him as LORD. After witnessing this, I knew there was so much more. I was not willing to let go till I saw Jesus on my campus. Something had to give.

I began to pray, "It doesn't matter if I'm the only one fully sold out to you GOD, I will seek your face, and I will come after you, your will and your ways. I will not be tainted by this place. I will embrace the believers."

I didn't know if there were any others feeling as I did. The good news was there were a few. I just prayed stupid prayers back then. Something had to change. I knew if there were others to join with in prayer and action, I would find them as I went forward.

One of them was of course "G-hoon" (Daniel Kim). The larger audience of InterVarsity and whatnot were partying, even the leaders. They were doing whatever they wanted with no thought of GOD or His ways, drinking, sex, drugs and more. There was no way of knowing if someone really loved Jesus or if they were half-hearted doing a Bible study one minute and out on the town hitting a bottle illegally the next. No offense to my friends that are reading this now, but it was what it was.

Along the way I'd hear stories of someone I'd come to know and love at one of the campus ministries I was a part of in high school would wind up scared they were pregnant, others were hooked on drugs and dealing with overdose scares. It just broke my heart. There was so much false Christianity. People wanted to look Christian but didn't want to pay the price to sell out all the way. There was so much immaturity; people did not control their fleshly desires so there was no way to raise the bar for unity and revival. Jesus was only real to people when they heard a guest speaker or as the worship band played songs during a service. Once they left the doors, there was no evidence of true living faith being demonstrated. It hurt inside as I struggled with people that only wanted to act like they were Jesus' followers when they were unwilling to change every part of their lives and completely sellout. I was a sellout. I sold it all on Jesus from the beginning. I do not think that was just something I did in and of myself. It was something GOD had done in me years before. Along with this call to full surrender was a call to purity, HE called me to stay a virgin until I was married. These two things just go together; you can't be one without the other. I took much ridicule for not sleeping around. If I could endure that, why would I back down for Jesus? It just strengthened the durability of my psyche.

3 HOPE WAS AT THE DOOR
FALL 1993

During one of those early days on campus, I prayed for God to give me hope, because I felt so alone. I was on the floor in my room praying "God, just give me hope, give me hope, give me hope, Lord, GOD, I just need hope, send hope." Just then there is a knock at my door at Hinton James on South Campus where I lived. I have to say right here, my roommate back then, Gene Hoffman was one of the smartest people I have ever known. This goes out to Gene. He was an amazing roommate to have during my freshman year even though he never saw eye to eye with me on faith. I learned so much from that guy and dearly miss him. So, I was there alone and praying when I heard the knock on the door.

I opened the door, and there's a young lady standing there and she says, "Hi, I'm Hope." I still get so tickled at this. Funny thing is I don't think I ever told her what had just taken place that day. It's so amazing that she came to the door at that exact time as a sign from GOD to me. I couldn't believe her name was "Hope!" I was like "You're kidding me." She says, "No, what?" We did this whole interchange, and I was like "Your name's Hope," and she goes, "Yeah, I'm with InterVarsity and I stopped by to see if you want to be part of a Bible study we're having here." I was like, "Oh, my stars, yeah." There was nothing to pray about. That had to be GOD. I started attending InterVarsity Bible study meetings immediately that week.

She never knew. I never told her but it's funny that I was praying for hope, and she knocked on the door. You pray, and God sends hope to knock on the door.

WATCH A CLIP HERE AS DUSTIN SHARES PERSONALLY ABOUT THIS PART OF THE STORY

INTERVARSITY & HEELS TO HEAVEN

It was only within a couple weeks after my joining InterVarsity campus meetings that it had started to really grow. There were a couple hundred people which was actually pretty big for those days. It was exciting, and people were with it. I sensed change.

Even still, I could tell it wasn't going to be like my church back home and what I had experienced with my high school youth group at South River where revival was stirred in the young people's hearts there. I had hopes that it would be something more. It was going to be so much more. I had no idea. It just wasn't even at the point when I first got there.

I made a lot of friends there. They asked me to be a part of a group called Heels to Heaven, which was a singing group. Within another week, I tried out for the group and made it in. My friends there whether I knew it or not, were partying, going out drinking even doing drugs; they were all about that scene. They would do the religious thing because it was what they knew and were accustom to. It was where they connected with people. I'm not putting anyone down. I loved the people and the group and enjoyed when we went and ministered in churches all over the state. It just grieved my heart to see people look so devoted to GOD and yet they were living a different life.

It's just, at these groups, it seemed like people used them as a way to connect with folks they could date with similar faith backgrounds. It wasn't about Jesus. People were not sold out. I was praying, God send revival to these campus meetings. I could feel there was nothing there. The people in attendance were hollow. Little did I know this was changing every day, God was working on their hearts.

And I don't want to harp on this through the whole book, but I need to make it clear for you, the reader if you are on a campus where GOD is not easily seen and has not moved yet, HE CAN MOVE and HE WILL USE YOU if you will allow HIM. There is more and no matter how bad it looks, it doesn't mean anything. It was at Asbury College in 1970 during uprisings on campuses around the US with demonstrations and turmoil that they saw revival hit. No matter how bleak it looks, do not allow that to determine what you believe about GOD and HIS WORD. Neither the culture around us nor our feelings should frame the TRUTH in the Bible. The Bible reframes and refreshes the culture and reality around us and it is bent into the making of GOD's reality. (Read the Warrior's Manual for more on this).

4 DANIEL KIM "CUT THE FAT…" FALL 1993

It was at Heels to Heaven that I first met G-hoon Kim. It would have been, I guess, the fall of 1993 that he actually came to one of the practices. We thought he was going to join the group. He came to instead preach and "cut the fat" as he called it; he dropped some word on us.

He came to do a major hard-core Bible study and call everyone to repentance. I knew the people in Heels to Heaven. I wanted to call them to repentance. I just didn't have the opportunity or know how. He came in and dropped this word on everybody. He called us out with his passionate teaching and moved many of us with his words and then he said, "I'm done." And that was it. He literally finished talking, gathered his things and walked right out of the room and out the door. I did not see him again for years. It was jaw dropping. I had never seen someone walk into a meeting, take a pulpit and microphone, speak with such authority and then simply walk out without an invitation, a prayer or anything else. I was blown away!!!!!

I remember thinking "Oh my goodness, that dude's got it. THERE IS SOMEONE ELSE!!!!! GRRRR!"

And there was. We just would not cross paths again for years! I did not know who he was, where he was or what he was doing. I just knew that I had to find him again someday.

That was the first time I saw someone absolutely on fire, like I was. I thought to myself "that's somebody I can hang with," and I really wanted to connect with him. I wanted to connect with him that night but then he disappeared. He jetted. He was gone.

CONVERSATIONS ON THAT FIRST INTERSECTION AT HEELS TO HEAVEN

(There is no better way to share this part than to share our actual conversation about our paths crossing at Heels to Heaven. What you will read from this chapter on is based on our actual conversation as we retell the story together).

Daniel Kim: Was that the first day I actually came?

Dustin: That was the first day you came to Heels to Heaven. You came in and it was like you were trying out or so we thought. You got up, spoke and left. You ripped us all a new one dude and just left. I said to myself, "Wow."

Daniel: I do remember saying some very aggressive words. I think at the time and especially in that particular season, the Lord really had a strong grip on my life. I was not very merciful to the half-hearted believers. In anger...I spoke because I knew the Lord was angry; it angered me too. Not that I am perfect, but to see half-hearted people doing things in the name of the Lord, but not out of true devotion to Him was really embarrassing. I do remember actually bringing my guitar. I think I even led some...

Dustin: You did a song?

Daniel: Yes, a song. Then afterwards, I think I just laid low. I said a few words. Then I remember packing up and leaving soon after.

So, from that day on, Daniel and I really parted ways. NOT ON PURPOSE. He just came and disappeared 007 style, which has always been his personality.

5 THE BASKETBALL CONNECTION
FALL 1993 TO SPRING 1994

Around that same time I connected with a young lady on the women's basketball team and we started going out. Of course, we were both believers and I had made a covenant to wait for my mate before doing anything physical, so let me say right here that nothing happened. We just went out. She was older than I and totally encouraged me in the faith.

I believe that I that Jill S_____ was placed in my life and used to urge me on for Jesus. She is the one that encouraged me to think about doing Bible studies, to speak up for GOD and do ministry. She played guitar and was outspoken for Jesus, too. She attended Fellowship of Christian Athletes and was always overtly talking about the Lord there.

She played on the women's basketball team -- amazing lady. She was one of a few people I ran into that I can say truly loved Jesus. She was different. She was one of the nicest, most creative people I have ever known, so kind and giving. I am thankful for GOD placing her in my life to urge me further in the faith. She was such a go-getter.

Some of my other friends, from Inner Varsity and Heels to Heaven, hung out and connected with Jill and the women's basketball team. These guys were primarily Randy Greene and Chris Bartlett. Jill invited us to the National Championship along with any friends and family that wanted to join since we watched the team play all season and supported them. We went to every single one of their games. We truly supported them even before they had a look at a National title for the NCAA.

A bunch of us guys ended up starting a fraternity called Chi Alpha Omega. It was crazy. I felt like GOD wanted me to start a Christian fraternity that would demonstrate the life of Jesus to the other fraternities on campus. I wanted it to be Christian men that would serve the community, demonstrate GOD's love to the other Greek organizations and treat women with respect and dignity. It became my mission. I had a couple fraternities that were trying to recruit me in their group because they heard that I played soccer but could not be on the varsity team, which meant that I could play for their club teams. So, they brought me to one of their big dinners and we ate steak, which was the best food you could get as a freshman in college!

After seeing a couple of their dinners and such, I thought to myself, this can be done better. I mean, we couldn't get a house and we didn't have as much support or finances as they did. But if we could just start getting people on board there was no telling what could happen in future years to come. I did not know how to start a fraternity. But I knew if I got enough people together and talked to the right leaders at school I just might have a shot at it.

Now, again, I did not know how to go about it, but I knew something had to be done. So, I researched and found out who was supposed to be over the Greek organizations on campus. I started to stalk that Dean (in the love of Jesus, Haha). I remember literally sitting outside of that Dean's door every single day to get his attention so I could get this thing started. I thought to myself, "If I just bother him enough, he is going to want to get rid of me and will finally do whatever it takes to get me to leave him alone." So, I became his shadow. I waited for him and talked to him every day as he came and went from his office, asking for the next steps. He told me to get a group of men together and have them sign a petition. I needed at least 30 men that would be in attendance the next semester and once I them and enough signatures; I could begin a charter. So, I got to work and started recruiting as well as continued pestering that Dean.

Before the fraternity even started, we were a brotherhood, meeting together, going to the women's basketball games together and supporting them at every game we could.

UNC WOMEN'S BASKETBALL

At this point, we figured that was our call on campus; literally just to support the women's basketball team until they were successful. Everyone supported the men's basketball program at Carolina. I mean, we had some of the most amazing men's players and were thought to be up for the national title that year back to back with the prior year. I remember going to the women's games and there were few in attendance with the exception of us. We were their support.

And boy did we support! WE WERE LOUD AND PROUD OF OUR WOMEN'S BASKETBALL. Little did we know that this was just leading us into alignment for the future.

That year the Women's Basketball Team ended up going to the National

Championship. They were really underrated and considered the underdogs. I remember how hard they had to work to get the ACC title. When they did get that title, they were ranked number four out of four number ones from each conference. They got down-seated. They struggled to get back to the top. They ended up in the National Championship game on Easter Sunday. Randy, Chris, my parents and I drove out to Richmond for that big playoff weekend.

The women played amazingly and Coach Sylvia Hatchell led like a champ. The entire coaching team, the players and more were an amazing lineup and they were doing it. They played right into the National Championship game despite not actually being picked to win. I remember some of the great players on that team were Charlotte Smith, Tonya Sampson, Marion Jones, and far too many more to name.

They were getting much less press than the boy's team which had Montross, Lynch, Wallace, Jamison and Stackhouse (which we knew from hanging out at the different campuses).

That Sunday morning I talked to Jill, I said, "I want to have a Bible study before Nationals with at least you and a couple others. I don't feel right not being in church on Easter Sunday." I never did anything exciting or crazy. I had never preached before. I had never done a Bible Study or even really taught for that matter except for when I would talk to people in my youth group or high school about the Lord. I prayed at church and I'd given my testimony, but that's about it. The only time I did anything really outspoken was when I spoke outside my high school at the "See You at the Pole Rally." So, this was a huge thing for me to even suggest leading something like this for a small group of people.

6 EASTER, THE UNC WAY
EASTER WEEKEND 1994

DUSTIN: I went to present the Bible study that morning. The topic for the day was on "doing everything as unto the Lord." I wanted to call the few of us that were together to literally die to ourselves like Christ did on the cross. I said that HE gave everything for us and the Father's glory. HE died and we can die to self. I felt like the Lord was calling the women to do everything as unto Him and that they should play that basketball game as unto the Lord. They should die to themselves and do it as a witness to Christ. God should get all the glory. They should be focused on the Lord even as they play basketball.

That was the topic. And in my head, I thought it would be spoken to about 5-10 people.

I went to go do that Bible study that morning. When I got in the doors, it wasn't just my three friends, my mom and dad, and a couple other friends (Randy Greene, Chris Bartlett my parents and Jill).

It ended up being the entire women's basketball team, Coach Sylvia Hatchell, and her coaching staff. Jill, rounded up the cheerleading team, the band, and their families. She literally got everyone that traveled there and was involved at any level along with the extended group of Carolina folks that were in the hotel to join us. She asked the hotel to reserve the main assembly/banquet hall for us all. They reserved the entire space!

I walked into this massive crowd of Carolina supporters thinking I was speaking to about 10 people, but Jill and Coach Hatchell had decided differently. It was everyone. We were all there in one accord. All of a sudden, it did not matter if some of those people did not know whether or not they believed in Jesus, in that moment, we were all united in belief and faith. All at once, we were together, united, prepared, listening and ready. I

28

could not believe it. I was overwhelmed in a matter of seconds as I realized what was happening and the fact that I was going to be the preacher for their Easter service. What an honor! And here is the kicker, Charlotte's dad an actual pastor and an amazing one at that was there. I felt so small. And yet, there we were, assembled for the greatness of GOD. We were a small group of David's and we faced a Goliath. Everyone innately knew that there was no way to get past this without some divine intervention and we were going to get some!

Even though there were better leaders and better preachers there, they deferred to us allowing Randy, Chris and I to lead some singing which we were trained to do from our time in Heels to Heaven. I said, "Randy, do a song." So Randy sang a song and led us in worship. We didn't even have a guitar. We were just singing with our voices, no instruments. And then I spoke. I did NOT speak well. I did NOT speak powerfully. I simply shared the Gospel and the heart of doing all things as unto GOD like Jesus had done in going to the cross. And that was it. However, in the weakness of the words, GOD was strong. And the Presence of GOD went through that place as hearts were emboldened. As I closed, Charlotte's dad, Reverend Smith stood and said that he wanted to back up what I had said and began to speak over all of us that this word from GOD we would accomplish and we would give glory back to GOD through this event.

Then we prayed and it was DONE! We closed up that thing, everybody was holding hands as we prayed then those women led us out to the ball game and played as unto the Lord. Easter had been celebrated and GOD had been placed FIRST! As we left, Coach Hatchell came over and pats me on my shoulder and says, "You're our Pastor today, Dustin..." "Thank you..." she never knew how much this meant to me nor did she know what she did inside my heart or how GOD used her that day.

It wasn't much. But it stuck. I never got over that. I think that was the first time I actually thought to myself, "Ministry... I can do this... GRRRR."

So when they hit that ball court, they were playing ball like madness. They really, really rocked out. I mean, they came out and put the other team back on their haunches. It was neck in neck the whole way with both teams taking leads at different points. The fact that the #4 ranked team was playing ball with the #1 team was huge.

At the very end of the game, Carolina's women's basketball team was two points down, they had like three seconds on the clock or whatever, and Charlotte Simpson says to the ladies, "Get the ball to me from across the court. I'm going to take a three-point shot."

It wasn't just a little three-point shot. It was a way-out there three-point, well beyond the range of a men's professional three-point shot, from the top of the half. So she threw that thing and got it, and they win the game by one point instead of tying at two.

It was crazy because she even stated she was going to do it for the Lord. Her dad was praying. Everyone was involved in praying. I was under my seat praying out loud to GOD for HIM to intervene.

I know, I know... Everyone prays at a ball games and GOD doesn't care... Well, that may be the case 99.9% of the time, however, I am convinced that when GOD can really get glory and can really be testified, sometimes he may intervene for something smaller that it not as big as ending world hunger. It all hinges on what HE wants to do and I believe GOD was arranging something. HE was aligning something we could not have expected. HE wanted to give these women a national title. HE wanted to give them the podium and platform on a national stage so that they could tell about Jesus and their playing for the LORD loudly. AND boy did they! HE wanted to unite our hearts. HE knew Coach Hatchell would one day be instrumental in playing a part in a future event we would have right there in her gym. HE knew. HE was at hand. And those are just a few things HE knew. HE also arranged a chance meeting with someone that sat near us. GOD did these things and so much more!!!!!

NATIONAL CHAMPIONS! GO JESUS!   ...That was the cry you could hear everywhere these ladies spoke.

After Nationals was over, every single lady basketball player interviewed whether on ESPN all the way to their interview while standing in front way the President when they were invited to the White House, they gave glory to God. They kept saying over and over and over, "We give glory to God.

After our meeting at the White House, Coach Hatchell and I had a great time talking off to the side of the bus, just before we got on, she says again, "Awesome job. Way to go. You're our preacher." That comment plays into the story later. Because of our conversation that day and her continually speaking into my life we connected forever. It's just one of those things God did back then.

CHANCE MEETING OR PURPOSED PLAN?

Now here is the interesting part. At that game, seated next to us was a guy named, Tony Shanks. I am not even sure how we got into the conversation, but he graduated from East Carolina University, and had been a part of a Christian fraternity there that already had a charter and could make the process infinitely easier. When he mentioned that, a light bulb clicked on inside my head.

Since he'd been involved during the early stages of starting a fraternity at ECU I told him how badly I wanted to start this fraternity at UNC Chapel Hill. He told me, "Get some guys together, make a plan, and go to the dean," he said once we did that we could use their charter because they had been a fraternity on a campus already. I told him I already had a group of guys and a list of names on a petition and that I had already been stalking the Dean of Student Affairs in order to get his attention. And there you have it, we were in business! It was amazing to see everything just align!

So, ba da bing, ba da boom, the following year we had a fraternity that would be used to witness to other fraternities on the campus at Carolina. I started the vision work for this fraternity and passed it off to my brothers. Chris Bartlett, Randy and I were the main leaders with a few others on the board for the first rushing class. Before we even started, I already knew that this was something they were to lead as I had more things to do for the Kingdom.

By the time I was in my sophomore year, I had been involved with Temple Baptist during the summer, which I will talk about next. So, I knew I could not be the President and Chris, after some arm twisting, stepped in to be the man. HE DID GREAT!

WATCH THIS CLIP AS DUSTIN SHARES SOME OF THIS STORY RIGHT FROM CARMICHAEL AUDITORIUM

7 DUSTIN ENTERS THE MINISTRY
SUMMER 1994

So, back to the summer of 1994, I had just completed my freshman year at school. I needed to do something to make money that summer, but I also wanted to be invested in GOD's work. I did not have any direction, but that was about to change quickly.

Tyler Jones, another brother on campus that was on fire for Jesus who I knew from Heels to Heaven, was about to lead me into the next phase of my life. He was invited to do a youth internship that summer with him somewhere I believe in Indiana where I think he was originally from. He asked me to join him. I thought it would be an amazing adventure; however, my folks did not like the idea of me being out of state for the entire summer. They decided to start to looking around for churches in North Carolina instead that may need a summer youth intern.

I really liked the idea of a summer internship because I had been deeply affected by a young lady named, Karissa Weir who had been my summer intern at South River Baptist Church. I wanted to be like her. She played an instrumental part in drawing me to follow Jesus in my freshman and sophomore years of high school. My youth pastor Tim was really complimentary of this idea; however, our friendship would soon be tragically separated. He would no longer be staying in ministry after that year. This was really another place where I felt knocked out of my comfort zone. I owe so much to Tim, the leadership at South River and so many others from that church and community. (And even though some of those people were split over what had taken place at that Church, I am still thankful for every person there from both sides of the divide. I have the capacity to say at this point in my life that you all have a part in the legacy GOD has left in my life. Thank you). You can see here, as GOD began doing more and more in my life and causing me to follow more and more after HIM, I faced different distractions that we all at times face that are setup to divide. It was hard to keep my eyes on Jesus, but I had nowhere else to look.

So, since I was still bent on doing ministry with Tyler and since my mom didn't want me going off far from home, which was North Carolina, she went full force into recruitment mode to find me something local. Mom ended up talking to a lady that volunteered at the school she had taught for many years (she actually taught me in that school when I was in kindergarten! She was and is an amazing teacher!) and she introduced me to Pastor Scott Pedersen. He was an enthusiastic, passionate young preacher at a small church in the area named, Temple Baptist Church.

Pastor Scott met with me. After interviewing me, he told me he had other people being considered for the job including someone that had done it the year before, but that he loved my heart for GOD. He said up front that he was willing to take a risk on me doing ministry despite no real experience because he saw the heart of David in me. That stuck, folks. These formative things would leave me ever changed. GOD was moving me into HIS will and HIS ways each step of the way. So, he hired me for the summer. I learned so very much. (Let me say here that I owe the Temple Baptist guys so much. You all allowed me to take risks and grow with you and your kids. I am who I am today because of your investment. I hope I am making all of you proud).

No one realized that this summer job would end up being my call into ministry for the long haul. I mean, Tim and Pastor Drum told me I was called to preach, but I did not know what that even meant. I did NOT want to be a pastor. That did not sound fun at all.

Also, Scott and Temple Baptist Church were the way I ended up meeting Dr. Henry Blackaby, getting involved in The Vineyard Movement, and being touched in Toronto by John and Carol Arnott and all those guys as well as becoming involved with Jack Taylor, attending Morningstar's Heart of David Conferences and Brownsville Assembly of GOD's revival. I even had the honor of meeting John Wimber and going on to later be on staff with Blood-n-Fire Ministries in Atlanta, Georgia. That was some kind of new fangled Kingdom seminary outside of seminary!

With that said, as I entered my sophomore year in college, I had been called to ministry. I could never have imagined that by the end of 1994 I would be licensed into ministry, who could deny it, I was called? It is not something that comes easy to be licensed, however, since I was already speaking in pulpits across the state as well as some other states on mission, my home church wanted to make sure they had licensed me officially into this ministry.

My uncle tried to get the pastor from his local Methodist Church to talk me out of going into ministry, thinking that I thought it was just a good job. After this pastor met with me, he told my uncle, "Yeah, the boy is called to minister…"

On December 4, 1994, I was licensed into full time ministry. I stayed on as the Youth Minister at Temple Baptist after the summer. It became my part time job on holidays, weekends and special events.

I drove two hours every Friday after class to Stony Point, NC to do ministry after classes and two hours back to school on Sunday nights late after evening service to go to back to college. This took me from campus and thus, my decision to have Chris be the president of our Christian fraternity even though I wanted to do it so badly. I just wouldn't be doing a service to this awesome fraternity by giving them my half-hearted attempts to lead and missing weekends and ministry and life with them. Not to mention, Chris was well up to the task as were all the guys. We were not perfect, but it was a START! We had a Christian Fraternity on campus and I was in ministry. Wow! Everything went so quickly.

During this 1993-1994 era, I ended up in youth ministry and founded a fraternity on campus that I ended up having to pass on to the larger Chi Alpha Omega leadership. Good times! I stayed a brother at Chi Alpha Omega. I just wasn't as active at the very end because I was busy about campus missions and Forest Fire. And I was as well, touched by the power and presence of God in Toronto, which is a whole other story.

8 DANIEL MAKES A DENT
ICA SPRING 1994

Dustin: So we had a couple years there where Daniel, at this point, I think '94, '95, and on it was out of the picture until we met up again after he had started ICA. (In Christ Alone Worship Team & Prayer Movement).

Before I really let Daniel jump into his story, I want so say a couple of things about this man that he will never say about himself. He is many generations descended from ancestors who did missional work in North Korea and South Korea as well as church planting in Europe and America. His ancestors were partially responsible for the awakening that hit North Korea many years ago before Communist rule. His father was a missionary church planter who planted in Belgium and America and still has a lasting legacy even though he is gone. He grew up in ministry with his brother. He was touched as a young boy, having had an encounter where GOD hit him with a fireball in a vision. Daniel "G-hoon" Kim may have seemed like just another ordinary servant of GOD at the time, but he had an extraordinary anointing, calling and heritage that GOD was about to bring to bear in this season. It was my honor to walk with him as well as to follow him in certain seasons as an older brother in the faith. I believe he dragged me along for a while just because the anointing that came on me was after I matured to become a good partner in ministry with him. When I met G-hoon, he was definitely in the lead in our 2x2 partnership.

So, here is more of his story as he hit UNC campus!

IN CHRIST ALONE
Daniel: A friend of mine Dan Tan whom I did not know at the time approached me. I remember he wanted to start a group or something so we could pray and unify the campus.

Dan was a very, very calm guy. Not charismatic at all, so for him to want to do something like this and to have already thought it through and pray about it was huge. To be honest, I don't exactly remember what drove him to reach out to me, but he did. I believe it was through some mutual connection.

We just met up one day and started talking and we both agreed that this is something of the Lord. We started praying. We didn't even start the group just then.

We just started praying together for a while. Then we came up with the name, In Christ Alone, out of the song, "In Christ Alone." This was the older song "In Christ Alone," not the latest one that is sung on the radio. I think it was sophomore year (1994-1995) when we started praying and then junior year (1995-1996) is when we actually, officially started In Christ Alone. ICA meetings.

Once ICA was established, we agreed to pray as a group weekly for the campus and to host a praise night on a monthly basis for all the campus ministries to join us in. The campus ministry was praise in the Pit, they called it, "Pit Praise," which was comprised of at least 5 campus ministries and sometimes many more. We felt like we had more of a leverage because we were the minority. (Our group was comprised of Korean and Chinese believers).

None of us belonged in any particular team or group. It was a way for us to say, "Hey, we're nobody and we're neutral, too. We just want everyone to come, and all we want to do is praise the Lord."

When we started doing that it was amazing because someone from the group was contacted by a guy named Chad at Wake Forest University through yet again a network of friends. This was pretty early on in our existence.

WATCH A CLIP WHERE DANIEL SHARES ABOUT ICA OUTSIDE GERRARD HALL ON CAMPUS

This is a poster from Pit Praise the year before Forest Fire 1997.

O FOR A THOUSAND TONGUES TO SING

O for a thousand tongues to sing
My great Redeemer's praise,
The glories of my God and King,
The triumphs of His grace!

Jesus! The name that charms our fears,
That bids our sorrows cease;
'Tis music in the sinner's ears,
'Tis life, and health, and peace.

He breaks the power of canceled sin,
He sets the prisoner free;
His blood can make the foulest clean;
His blood availed for me!

My gracious Master and my God,
Assist me to proclaim,
To spread through all the earth abroad
The honors of Your Name!

O for a thousand tongues to sing
My great Redeemer's praise,
The glories of my God and King,
The triumphs of His grace!

ONE NAME

✧   One name, under heaven
Whereby we must be saved.
One name, under heaven
Whereby we must be saved.

Searched for a long long time
Searched both night and day
Then somebody showed us
That Jesus is the way! He's that... ✧

Forgiven of my sin
Baptized in water
Filled with the Holy Ghost and
Washed in the blood of the Lamb!
By that... ✧

God's gonna move this place,
God's gonna move this place,
God's gonna turn this campus
Upside-down! By that... ✧

Free, really free, my friend
Freed by the blood of the Lamb
Free, really free, my friend
Freed by the blood of the Lamb
He's that... ✧

SHINE, JESUS, SHINE

Lord the light of your love is shining
In the midst of the darkness, shining;
Jesus, light of the world, shine upon us.
Set us free by the truth You now bring us.
Shine on me, shine on me.

✧   Shine, Jesus, Shine,
Fill this land with the Father's glory.
Blaze, Spirit, blaze.
Set out hearts on fire!
Flow, river, flow.
Flood the nations
With grace and mercy.
Send forth your word,
Lord, and let there be light.

Lord, I come to your awesome presence,
From the shadows into Your radiance;
By the blood I may enter Your brightness.
Search me, try me,
consume all my darkness.
Shine on me, shine on me. ✧

As we gaze on your kingly brightness,
So our faces display Your likeness:
Ever changing from glory to glory.
Mirrored here may our lives tell Your story.
Shine on me, shine on me. ✧

WE EXALT THEE

For thou oh Lord art high
Above all the earth
Thou art exalted far above all gods
(Repeat)

We exalt thee
We exalt thee
We exalt thee
Oh Lord
(Repeat)

WHO DO YOU SAY THAT I AM?

I turned water to wine,
And they called me magician.
I gave sight to the blind,
And they called me physician.
But what about you? What about you?

✧   Who do you say that I am?
Who do you say is the Son of Man?
Do people see, what you believe?
Who do you say that I am?

I told them the trut
And they called m
I healed and forga
But that was not th
But what about you

(BRIDGE)
I am the Way
Truth and the
Those who kn
But what abou
What about yo

YOU ARE MY AL

You are my strengt
You are the treasur
You are my all in al
Seeking You as a p
Lord to give up I'd t
You are my all in all

✧   Jesus, Lamb
Worthy is Yo
Jesus, Lamb
Worthy is Yo

Taking my sin, my c
Rising again; I bless
You are my all in all
When I fall down Yo
When I am dry, You
You are my all in all

Above is a song sheet that was used for Pit Praise. The team would have hundreds of these printed front and back and would hand them out to people as they came up to listen so that they could sing as well since not everyone knew the words.

WATCH A CLIP OF DUSTIN STANDING AT THE PIT, TELLING THE STORIES OF PIT PRAISES THAT TOOK PLACE THERE.

TRAGEDY STRIKES
January 1995

Dustin: You know, I would say, to kind of even frame this time period at Carolina, it was 1995. There were all these fractured campus groups. They were starting, but I don't think it had the reach partially because people were half-hearted, you know? It was like G-hoon was saying; there was a lot of half-heartedness.

I will never forget January 26, 1995, a guy by the name of "Wendell Williamson," walked out near Franklin Street and began to shoot the street up. He shot a number of people including a police officer that lived. He ended up killing one of our athletes at the school.

It affected the heart of the school. It truly, deeply affected me. And if affected the desperation that I felt as I went forward praying. This was part of my drive for intimacy and for revival on campus. The day that this tragedy happened, I had come out of Alumni Hall and I remember as I was walking out I thought to myself, "hey it may be cold, but it's a nice day out maybe I should just walk back to Hinton James…"

Immediately after thinking this I thought, "I never walk back all the way to South campus from Alumni Hall. It's a good size walk. I can just ride the bus for cheap or free. I'm just gonna hop on the bus."

I had this interaction in my head. I was just learning how to hear GOD. It was a strange time for me. I was learning how to discern the voice of God. I thought to myself, "Why am I arguing with myself about riding a bus?"

During this conversation inside my head it dawned on me since this thought is not within my normal range of thinking I should just walk back because it's probably God. I kept thinking, maybe it's GOD having me do this.

It was very quick. It was a nonchalant. It was not a big deal really so I decided to just walk back from Alumni Hall. I apparently was about halfway across campus when shots were fired; however, I did not hear anything otherwise I would have run back up there. (My natural reaction to problems and accidents is to run and help. It's weird. But I have a history of being the first to help on a scene. If I had heard this, I would have run to it, not from it). I did not hear a thing all throughout my walk.

As I made my way to my college dorm, people came busting out of their dorm rooms. Apparently they knew something I didn't. Since it's such a long walk, by the time I made it back, the shooting was literally on the news not as everything was playing out, but media was on the scene reporting what had happened. People were screaming. It was mass mayhem. I'd never seen anything like it in my entire life.

People were running in pandemonium and screaming and crying and running out in the middle of the open streets, which wasn't wise. They should have stayed indoors where it was safer. They ran. The whole dorm was hemorrhaging people who were scattering wildly around.

As they're running around me, one of my friends, Danielle, comes and runs and grabs my neck and she says, "Oh my gosh, you're OK. I knew you were up there. I thought it was you." I said, what are you talking about?

What did you think happened? She said, "There was a shooting. I knew you were up there on North Campus."

WATCH A CLIP AS DUSTIN SHARES WHILE STANDING NEAR WHERE HE WAS THAT DAY

You guys, I literally came out of Alumni Hall and I was going to the same bus stop that I always go to and that was the bus stop that was in the middle of the shooting and got all shot up. I would have literally been there the moment everything happened, but God had sent me another way. It was a couple hundred yards away from where I had my mental debate.

That did something on our campus. It did something in me. For a while I wondered why I had been spared. It didn't make sense to me and so many of my friends felt the same way. We were affected. We could not shake it. It truly, truly affected our campus all together. In general, everyone had been affected. Since this was an athlete, he was in Fellowship of Christian Athletes. Fellowship of Christian Athletes wasn't very large back then.

I remember, I believe it was Anne Graham Lotz' brother-in-law that was Coach Lotz, who was over FCA back then. Anne Graham, was either wife or she was sister-in-law or something; Anne Graham is, of course, Billy Graham's daughter. She did not come for that tragedy, she just came to minister.

When I spoke with her during this whole time period, she would really speak into me, well all of us. It was a great covering at that time at Carolina. In the middle of this brokenness, there was such grieving. It was a good thing to see everyone come together.

9 THE FIRE IS IGNITED
FALL 1995

Daniel: Chad wanted to gather a large group of InterVarsity students that was fairly active at Wake Forest University. He wanted to do a praise night. He heard about us and wanted us to come and lead the worship. (It would be an event called "Forest Fire" based on spreading fire of GOD at Wake Forest University).

That's actually what we went to do. We didn't go there with any intention to organize anything. We went there to lead the worship. However, we also got to play a part in helping Chad organize the event and bring everything together.

After this event at Wake Forest University, I don't remember how it happened, but we all felt like we should do a worship night at UNC Chapel Hill as well. This opens up to the next chapter.

By the way, I heard about Duke's large group and I couldn't believe it!
There till 2:30 am. You were there weren't you! Praise God.

* *
* * * * * * * * * * * * * * * * * * *

How It All Began

"Consider what a great forest is set on fire by a small spark."
(James 3:5b)

The name Forest Fire has special meaning. Both of the words
"forest" and "fire" communicate the history and the meaning of this
annual praise night. "Forest" comes from Wake Forest University where
the vision of Forest Fire was born on March 30, 1996. The word "fire" is
the goal of the praise night--to set people's love for God aflame in
their hearts. Forest Fire is now a statewide movement in North Carolina
that is led entirely by students in their desire to see change on their
campuses.

At the time, Wake Forest students had a lot of social and
spiritual barriers between them. The campus was characterized by its
pretty outward appearance of the buildings and the people. It was
difficult to show weakness and be real with struggles. This stifling
atmosphere crept into the Christian fellowships as well. people felt dry
in their relationships with God, and inspiration was almost null. This
is not what God had intended for his people. In the book of Acts, we see

communities filled with the Holy Spirit who are bonded together through their common focus of Jesus Christ. They worshipped together, shared possessions together, and proclaimed the love of Christ together. Wake Forest was in dire need of rejuvination in their faith on Christ. They needed to see God's power and love in an awesome way.

God brought together a group of students on the campus who discovered this need and began to pray together. Chad ▬▬▬▬, a sophomore, felt the burden in the fall of 1995. He attended the Caemon's Call concert at Duke University where people praised God right in the middle of the quad on a Friday night! He thought, "Why couldn't WE have this?" He also attended their InterVarsity large group the next week where there was a lot of caring love. Both events drew all races together, proving that unity is powerful. Ephesians 2:14,18 says, "For he himself is our peace, who has made the two one and has destroyed the barrier, thedividing wall of hostility...for through Him we both have access to the Father by one Spirit."

From there, Wake Students got into contact with leaders from InChrist Alone who provided monthly praise nights to unify and renew students in the Raleigh-Durham area. In his hometwon of Chicago, IL, Chad also had the opportunity to experience city-wide praise nigths in a multi-ethnic community. Through mutual prayer and accountability, ICA began to work jointly with Wake Forest students in planning Forest Fire '96.

Gradually, all elements of the event were provided by God. The place, the money, the speaker (Clayton King), and the amazing friendships built between Asains, whites and blacks were all established in the preparation stage.

The event lasted four hours as the 500 person crowd listened to student speakers and the stirring testimony of Clayton King who spoke of Christ's love in John 8. The worship broke down walls between students and God, and between students themselves. They saw Jesus as one who "sympathized with [their] weaknesses" and one who gives "mercy and grace in time of need" (Heb 4:16). 40 students rededicated their lives their lives and/or accepted Christ into their hearts. People could not stop hugging each other afterwards. The effects are still ingering at Wake Forest as Christians from diverse backgrounds are praying more and more

in unity. The Spirit is moving others to start more Bible studies, prayer groups, and outreach events as well.

This year, the event traveled to Chapel Hill after careful consideration and prayer. The Triangle region is one of the nation's most influential areas academically where over 50,000 students attend college. This year is has the opportunity to unleash Forest Fire on them!

God has his grasp on Wake forest, and will reclaim North Carolina as a whole as his Spirit moves. Always remember that God can use a small spark to get a fire going.

Even before the Forest Fire 1997 event came along at UNC we were very, very faithful. That is one thing I can say with confidence. We had been faithfully praying on a weekly basis. Many of us actually met together in a smaller setting, either by two's or three's and we prayed even more for each other and for the group, for the campus.

Every month, I remember the Lord was growing the number of attendance at monthly praise nights. It was getting stronger. It was becoming very spiritual. The Lord was coming down and meeting us at our praise nights. There was a real tangible sense of God's goodness there. We were all getting blessed. That was the beginning of ICA.

10 FRAMING EXPECTANCY
WINTER 1995

Heading into my sophomore year, I met Henry Blackaby at an Experiencing God Conference. I asked him what advise he'd give a young person that was going into ministry and preaching the gospel. At this point, even in my sophomore year, I'd started speaking on the campus. I'd preach at the Pit, in open spaces, and would witness to anybody I could and pray for anybody I could.

He said to me, don't be a mediocre preacher. We don't need any more mediocre preachers. We have too many of them on the planet. He said, be the one man who is sold out entirely to the cause of Christ. He goes on to say read about the greats. Read about every great you can find. Read about George Whitfield, Charles Finney, and Jonathan Edwards.

Read about all of the greats through history, all the great revivals and awakenings, the people who saw God move, do what they did right. Don't do what they did wrong, and then go get the book by Oswald Chambers "My Utmost for His Highest," and read it.

He said, "Read that every day." He said, "Do that, because that's where I got my stuff from." And he didn't even tell me to keep reading "Experiencing God" even though "Experiencing God" had radically framed my understanding of how to do day-to-day life as a Christian. We can experience God day-to-day. It was a normal thing. And so, I did it. And I had read Power Evangelism by John Wimber as well as some of George E Ladd's work and it totally tuned me into the Kingdom's collision in the now. My readings about Evan Roberts and the Welsh revival stirred me deeply and the way they prayed for 100,000 souls. And at this point, someone sent me a video of Asbury 1970 Revival where Dennis Kenlaw is sharing the stories and what he and the students experienced there. THAT

VIDEO MESSED ME UP!!!!!

I actually went back to Carolina and looked everywhere I could to find information on revivals. I went to every library even going into Iredell County to research revival history. I even found a local history for revivals. I found out about our protracted meetings in the Fourth Creek or Third Creek area.

I found out about all kinds of stuff during the Great Awakenings and even what happened with Concord Presbyterian Church, how it was split during the Awakenings, and the old lights and the new lights split off. I even found out tons of stuff about the local area and UNC.

I read every single book on revival or movements of God on the third floor at the library. I'm talking about shelves and shelves, rack after rack, I read them all. Not one left. I spent every free moment that I was not in the closet or in class or ministry there reading and copying information. I have piles of writing and journals as well including the timeline I have added to the back of this book from my times spent there. I couldn't find anything else to read so I started looking around some of the old stacks, and old libraries, papers, and everything else.

WATCH THIS CLIP AS DANIEL AND DUSTIN RETRACE STEPS THROUGH THE UNC LIBRARY WHERE DUSTIN READ ABOUT THE GREATS FOR HOURS A DAY

I hunted everywhere I could think of, and I could not find anything else, until I found a bunch of old books sold at the front area of Davis Library, in a box. It was here that I bought some original old, old revival writer's books, first editions that were no longer around. I still have those today.

They came from personal libraries, from whatever, donated to UNC libraries, that they got rid of because they no longer wanted them in their personal library collections, not realizing what they had. But I was able to get them. So I read all these revivalists and all these writers.

SURROUNDING OURSELVES WITH PASSIONATE

FRIENDS

At this point, I've been thoroughly affected by the Vineyard having been touched, back in 1994, I believe it was, at Toronto, where God knocked me down and ruined me. I first had visions and encounters, and that was after not believing that God did that stuff. I actually went to prove it wrong.

Then there were interactions where every chance we got we went to revival meetings, whether it was to Melbourne, Florida, to the Tabernacle, or to meetings in Greensboro, that we would run home to, just me, or friends, or whoever. We would go out to any place where we heard that "Morning Star" was doing something.

I was attending "The Heart of David" conferences, going to every meeting where the Presence of God would show up. I saw and heard so much. And then we found out about the "Brownsville Revival" in 1995 in Florida and the awakenings in South America. So, we chased Claudio Friedzon and Carlos Annacondia when they were in the states as well as John Wimber, Randy Clark, Steve Hill, Lindell Cooley and anyone that could teach us more or where we could be refilled. We wanted anyone and everyone to place their hands on us and pray for us and they did. Randy Greene and I began to chase these guys during this time. We went anywhere we could find young people on fire like us. Whatever it took to stay in love with Jesus and hang with passionate worshipers.

I went down there so many times it's unbelievable. Randy and I kept driving down. I remember being there during spring break in '97. This was at the very end of us being at Carolina and actually after Forest Fire and was one of many times I had been there since 1995, but I'm going to skip ahead, only because it's one story that really rocks out about Brownsville.

The week of Spring break at UNC and all the surrounding campuses when people typically went to Pensacola, Florida to party, we all went down to be at Brownsville Assembly of God. Fourteen thousand students showed up at Brownsville Assembly of God. There wasn't enough room for them. There was only room in the main area for 1,200 or so people. The overflow had overflow rooms in various locations in different class rooms; some held 100 people, others 400. The biggest I do believe was 800. It was a big facility, but still not nearly enough room for all who came.

They had to put Jumbo-tron screens, and I mean jumbo Jumbo-tron screens, outside on the grass. People were sitting in the grass and all the way back into the parking lot watching them. The presence of God was heavy and people were receiving ministry and were being saved, healed and delivered after service in the parking lot, on the ground while in the Presence of GOD. Just seeing people hungry for Jesus like this leaves a mark. You are never the same. You are either scared away by the passion or you are overwhelmed with revelation of the greatness of GOD and never the same.

We saw all those students come out from three in the morning to get in the doors at 6:00 PM at night, because the glory of God was so strong. People would run into the building to get a seat. That's right, they would run into the building.

The line to get in the building went around the entire parking lot and down the side street, down past the church and down the road. Can you believe it, down the road to get into a church service?

They had church services every night except for Tuesday, when they would have a prayer meeting. They would have thousands come out to their prayer meetings at Brownsville Assembly of God, the presence of God was so strong.

All these things affected us, along with connecting with the Billy Graham Evangelistic Association and the Billy Graham Crusade that came to Charlotte, being trained in discipleship by their group, being stirred up in all these different ways. All of this stuff was playing into our passion and our excitement both as we headed into doing the event at UNC as well as what was to take pace afterwards when we were catapulted into ministry around the state and nation and soon, the world.

I was sitting and learning from Harry Bizzell up at the Mountain, in Moravian Falls after being introduced by Pastor Scott. Hanging out with Don Potter. These amazing people were speaking prophetic words. We're high-fiving Randy Clark in the hallways while we're there hearing conferences.

GOD was really moving in revival power with my youth group at Temple as well as just stirring things to the next level. Everything was coming together for something BIG!

WATCH THIS CLIP AS DUSTIN SHARES ABOUT SURROUNDING YOURSELF WITH THE RIGHT PEOPLE

Dear Richard Riss:

I would like to share with you what God is doing at Temple Baptist Church, Stony Point, NC, where I am the pastor.

God Bless,

Scott

This is a brief update on what God is doing at Temple Baptist Church!

Our youth group went to "Prayer Mountain" on Sept. 14 in Moravian Falls, NC, otherwise known as Apple Hill Lodge, to pray for an upcoming revival service that they were leading at a Southern Baptist Church on Sept. 20-21. They started praying at 5:30 PM Saturday evening and stopped at 5:30 AM Sunday morning. God strongly fell on that mountain from 2:30 - 5:30 AM. Many of the youth were on the ground (literally in the dirt and on rocks and wood) under the power of the Holy Spirt. Some were shaking and others were receiving gifts of the Spirit. All of them were visited by an angel. I have since learned that many who pray on this mountain see angels. Their lives were radically changed! The revival services were great. Two were saved and many prodicals came home! Thank you, Lord! He answers prayer and is always faithful.

What an awesome service we had this past Sunday morning (Sept. 22)! God came by and visited us for more than two hours. The Spirit was strong in the place before the service even started and no one wanted to leave when we closed at 1:00 PM. We had Baptism and Lord's Supper. People were flooding the alter during the Lord's Supper, worship, preaching, and invitation. There were many people broken before God. Some were testifying and prophecying. Others were interceeding and groaning and moaning in the Spirit!

We had several guests with us. Mr. & Mrs. Harry Bizzell (Apple Hill Lodge - Moravian Falls, NC), Mr. & Mrs. Buck Petty (Moravian Falls, NC), and Mr. & Mrs. Don Potter (Nashville, TN). Don Potter leads worship for Rick Joyner's Conferences in Charlotte. Don is a precious man of God. Don gave a prophetic word for our church and young people. He challenged the church to accept the anointing that God was pouring out on our young people and not to be jealous. We are not to hinder or restrain this anointing in any way but encourage and bless what God is doing. The Spirit of God fell as he prayed for the youth! Youth fell on their knees in brokenness, one fell under the power, others interceeded aloud, and still yet others cried, groaned, and moaned in the Spirit!! People flocked to the alter for prayer. So much more happened. It is impossible to put everything in words. Thank you, Lord! We pray for MORE!

We had a scheduled Deacons Meeting on Monday. They were ALL rejoicing and praying for the Lord to do more! Hallelujah!

Larry Booth, pastor at First Baptist Church, Satellite Beach, Florida, will be speaking this coming Sunday morning (Sept 29). Larry is very involved in the Melbourne Renewal ever since it broke out in January 1995! He is a precious friend and leader in renewal! The Lord is going to move again powerfully this Sunday morning!! Thank you Jesus!

We are having Renewal Services October 27-30, 1996. Lee O'Hare, pastor of New Beginnings Vineyard, and Jeff Rowland, pastor of Gospelway Baptist Church (Independent), and others will be speaking. All of the speakers are moving in this renewal! Very excited. Anticipating and expecting great things! Dustin, an evangelist on staff at Temple, prophecied to me that things were going to break loose even prior to the Renewal Services. They are happening! Yes, Lord!

All to the glory of Jesus Christ! Yes, Lord, Yes, We Will Ride With You!! Even So, Lord, Come!!
J. Scott Pedersen

Hello,

My name is Mike Conroy. I'm a member of Brownsville Assembly of God.

I am helping to answer some of the E-Mail. If you have more questions after this reply please contact the brownsville E-mail address again brownsville.AG@pen.net

Received your e-mail about Forest Fire 97.

We have placed your request on the prayer table. May God bless Forest Fire 97

Mike Conroy

And hearing John Wimber speaking changed my entire thinking about what GOD could do as the Kingdom of GOD was able to break into our reality now just as before, which built on what I had learned from Henry Blackaby. I actually read every book Wimber had written in a very short period of time. I actually listened to every tape he had that I could get, even dating back in the '80s before he was Vineyard, whenever he's speaking at James Robison's stuff with a bunch of the guys like Jack Taylor and hanging with Peter Lord.

We hung out with Jack Taylor. We hung out with all these guys. It was amazing back in these days. They were stirring. G-hoon had come from a history of revival in South Korea. He had history from his heritage, his dad all the way up to his great-grandparents. God had been moving in our lives and stirring us up to this point.

I add this because if you are out there reading this and you are wanting to see GOD move, don't just sit still, go wherever you have to and find people stirred up who are loving Jesus and join them. Learn from them. Get a crowd of GODly counsel around you. Do not go it alone. Go wherever GOD is moving and have it!!!!!!

We had heritage. We had literally all of this history, all this truth, all this expectancy, and then we headed that into the campus.

ASBURY 1970

The video recording of the Asbury 1970 revival rocked my world. I showed it to all my kids at youth. I showed it to everyone I could. I actually met one of the people who lived in Stony Point, North Carolina, who was there at Asbury in 1970. He told me, "Pray. Pray daily for your campus." This was before started working on Forest Fire but after I had already started praying with others on campus. This made me get more specific and strategic, and that brother told me "to pray daily for my campus."

WATCH THE EXACT VIDEO THAT SO AFFECTED US RIGHT HERE

I started praying daily, just like Asbury. I got two other guys together, and we would pray every day in the open air area. They were Brendan Irwin and Mike Peters. These brothers were amazing! It was in the amphitheater at Carolina. We were praying for a revival at Carolina.

The last prayers there were after I met G-hoon, and it was leading into Forest Fire, but we were praying that GOD would even overflow a movement across the campus that would fill up every campus ministry to the hilt. That there'd be excitedness in every student, and that even the amphitheater would be overflowed with GOD's Presence and movement on the campus. Which I want to say, at this point, that did happen by Spring 1997 after the Forest Fire event.

After Forest Fire, Campus Crusade actually outgrew Gerard Hall and couldn't meet in it. They had to meet outside in the amphitheater with almost a thousand students all the way up the hills to the road. It was amazing.

I was there to see it. When I found out about it, I thought to myself, "I've got to be there. That's what I prayed for in this very place for years now." And I got to watch as my prayer was answered.

Anyway, back to the story. I just want to frame with all this stuff that played in over the top of this stirring up of revivals, this hope for GOD to move, even seeing GOD move at Temple with the youth kids.

11 THE CLOSET AND THE COUCH
SPRING OF 1995 AND FALL 1996

It was in that moment that I realized we have to come together. We had to come together. It was as if at some point I had to become a missionary to this campus. I really pressed in during prayer. By this time I was really into worship. I had been touched at Toronto Airport Vineyard Christian Fellowship and the powerful renewals that were happening there and at the Vineyard while I was attending conferences. At Temple Baptist, we had a true revival spreading especially in the young people. We were on fire. We were doing ministry, missions, dramas and more. And GOD would come as we prayed and the Presence of GOD was tangible. It was thick.

As a result of being touched by those times of worship, I would often go back to my room at the Green House after class during my Junior year and just get in the presence. On any given day you could guarantee at some point, I would lock myself up in my room and get down on the floor with just notes of handwritten songs because I couldn't afford a cd player back then and just worship. (I had moved from Hinton James during my junior year of college).

I would just take notes, paper notes at conferences while the singers sang. I would write down every lyric as fast as I could for the worship songs because I had never heard anything like this before. When we sang, my insides opened up and I felt fuller. I felt alive and awake. Hope would fill my lungs, my heart would leap. GOD felt real. HE came near. HE inhabited the praises of HIS people. And all I could think is that I had to have that every day. I could not wait for the next meeting. I had to get down on my knees, weep and sing as HE came over me. So, I would get down on my knees and just pray and worship God in my room and ask Him to come, like at the meetings where I'd seen Him.

His Presence would come in the rooms where I was at. He came in the dorm room for the first part of my sophomore year, or the end of my sophomore year. He came in my room that I had at the "Green House" in my junior year.

The Green House (this is the name of the place where I lived during my Junior and Senior years) was a house that was bought by one of the InterVarsity moms over the years. Her son had graduated but she kept renting it out to InterVarsity guys. It is located off of Franklin Street and the cross street there not far from University Mall. I grew more there than anywhere in my entire life. The Prayer Closet at that house will always be the most special to me. It is where GOD first came to meet me. And HE CAME IN POWER!

WATCH AS DUSTIN SHARES ABOUT THE PRAYER CLOSET IN FRONT OF THE GREEN HOUSE

I was staying at a room at this point in my junior year. I would get down on my knees there as well and just worship. I'd sing old songs by John Wimber like, "Isn't He". Some of my other favorite songrwriters and worship leaders were David Ruis, Carl Tuttle, Brian Doerksen, Andy Park, and John & Marie Barnett. I especially loved singing songs like "Jesus, Holy and Anointed One". "Holy and Anointed One" was one of my favorites as was "Arms of Love" and "Remember Mercy."

"This Is the Air I Breath" by John and Marie Barnett was another songwriting couple I loved. those guys were amazing. I literally remember thinking about how cool it would be to just have time with those guys. I'd be on my knees singing their songs along with different songs of Carl Tuttle and Danny Daniels.

I would just keep singing these old Vineyard songs over and over and over again on my knees. Seeking God and asking GOD's Presence to come in that era on our campus. Asking God to unite things. I sang those worship songs, I ate the WORD of GOD even more than my text books. This is when I first read the Bible through and through and now it is something I do often. I went deep into studying Oswald Chambers' book,

"My Utmost for His Highest," and Henry Blackaby's books, "Fresh Encounter" and "Experiencing GOD." I read everything I could find on all of the greats in the UNC library. I WAS HUNGRY! And that hunger was a gift. We need to ask for it again.

It was at this time that me and two friends started meeting every week, twice a week on Tuesdays and Thursdays to pray for revival on campus. Brandon and Mike were amazing prayer warriors and we would meet, pray together before classes at Forest Theater and then spend the next 30 minutes to an hour walking around the theater and praying out loud, begging GOD to come. We actually began to pray for GOD to so grow revival on campus that groups would have to overflow their meeting rooms and would be forced to meet at Forest Theater. (This actually took place at that exact place my senior year after Forest Fire. INSANE!)

LISTEN TO DUSTIN SHARE ABOUT THAT STORY FROM IN FRONT OF FOREST THEATER

Revival had been breaking out at Temple Baptist Church, which is a whole other story. GOD had been doing a lot of stuff heading into my junior year. So, ending my junior year, I remember thinking I had to do more. I couldn't just be a youth pastor and I couldn't just be a half-hearted student. I had to see GOD do something GOD-sized at UNC. It had to happen.

When I came back for my senior year, (1996-1997) I wanted to be a campus missionary. There was not title or staff role for this. It is what GOD spoke to my heart so I asked my pastor at that point, Pastor Scott to send me out as a missionary to that campus. I wanted to be what I called an intercessory prayer missionary. I had never heard the term or concept. It was spoken into my soul.

I was called to reach my campus with revival. To me revival looked like students that said they were Christians getting passionate for Jesus and reaching the lost who had never heard the Gospel and as a result their coming to know Jesus.

As I ended my summer after my junior year with Temple, I resigned after a couple years being with them as their youth minister, to be this campus intercessory prayer missionary, or campus missionary at UNC Chapel Hill.

All I knew I could do is pray every day. Every hour I had free, I had to devote to concerted, specific, prayer. I could fast. I could seek the Lord. I needed to get a place that was specific for prayer. So when I came back to campus, I told the guys that I wanted to trade my bedroom, the place where I locked the door and spent time alone learning to worship, the place that meant so much to me and not only that, my bed, for a closet. Yes, I wanted to trade my room that I had shared with another guy for the closet in the hallway.

THE CLOSET AND THE COUCH

They thought I was crazy. They said, "So, you're gonna give up your bed in the bedroom and let us rent it out to someone else? You're gonna keep paying your same rent, sleep on the couch, and take the closet?" (I kept my clothes in a bag).

I was like, "yup." So I did. They let me have the closet. I painted that closet. I got it set up. I had it hooked up. I rewired a receptacle into it. I finally got a cd player that was given to me by my pastor. I got it all in there. Got it set up with my old computer speakers. I had everything in that space. I put pillows on the ground to kneel and had names and prayer requests taped all over the walls.

On the back wall it said "Enter to worship." On the door it said "Exit to serve." (Kermit Harpold a sign-maker/pastor and a father in the faith gave it to me for the closet. He supported me and spoke into my life as I went through this season).

You saw those words when you were coming in and going out.

Kermit's daughter, Summer Harpold and I, had become very close friends while I was at South River a few years before. Kermit, after meeting back then said he knew that there would be more for me to do for GOD. He, Becky (his wife) and Summer began to invest in me and invited me to sleep on their couch and do ministry with them. They had been speaking into me for a couple years by this point. It was all coming together.

Temple Baptist Church, the Harpold's and a couple others were really encouraging me in this prayer thing. Others thought I was crazy, weird and too zealous. So I prayed. I prayed every moment I had free. I became an intercessory prayer missionary praying for revival. I prayed for hours a day. I mean hours. If I didn't pray four hours, I would stay up into the night until I had prayed more than four hours.

I had a habit of witnessing. I had to witness to multiple people every day. It was just something that was built into me. As a matter of fact, I didn't feel right unless I led somebody to Jesus every day. It was just bizarre. Sometimes I would have to get back up off the couch and go out and tell someone about Jesus at the gas station that was open or on the street. I could NOT get loose from this drive of the Spirit. All I wanted was to simply be obedient. So, if I felt stirred, it didn't matter if I was on or not, I had to go!!!!!!

Whether or not I got it pulled off didn't matter. It was what I was about. I led tons of people to Jesus within no time. I was an evangelist and a prayer warrior. I still feel this way today. It's why I cannot quit witnessing and praying. Maybe some of you who know me are starting to understand why I am so excited about Jesus.

This leads me to this piece where it all comes together. One day I was on campus in the fall of my junior year. It was early on. I'd just gotten back. I saw a flyer from the prior year, which tells me it was very early on.

I believe it was at Carroll Hall. It was stuck on the wall. It said ICA, all campus praise. I thought, "what is this?" It was from the last semester. God told me, rip it down off the wall and take it with you. I said to myself, "whatever." I ended up taking it and I stuck it in my prayer closet. I thought; "well, at least I can pray for them. I'll pray for this group ICA. I will pray God blesses them and that He does bring the campus ministries together. They're doing it. Let's pray it in."

I started praying for them every day. One day, while I'm in my prayer closet, I got a very definitive word for one of the guys who was named on that poster. His old phone number was on it. His name was Dan Tan.

God spoke to me three things; He said, number one, tell Dan that I am taking care of his finances, not worry about it. I will take care of his studies, and not to worry about that either. Lastly, he will see revival. It was in that kind of wording. It was very directive, like he will see revival on this campus at UNC.

I thought, "OK." I didn't know if Dan was praying for those specific things or not. I got on the phone. Here I'm a young, young, guy, I guess, I'm not a young Christian at this point. Been a Christian since I was a kid, but I was young in my hearing God phase. I got on the phone, called the phone number, and low and behold, it still worked. He kept the same phone using the same number and living in the same place he was last semester, which did not always happen.

I said, "Dan." He said, "Yeah." I said, "You don't know me. My name is Dustin Hedrick, but I need to tell you something, and you just need to listen. God says," ...and I told him the three things.

Now, I've learned since then, you probably shouldn't say "God says." There's better ways to put it, but I was very young then, so I gave him a directive.

When I got done, I didn't even give him space to tell me if I was right or wrong. I was ready to get off that phone. I remember thinking, "All right man. Blessings," and I was just ready to go. Dan is like, "No, wait. What's your name?" I said, "Dustin." He said, "What's your phone number?" I told him. He says, "I'll call you back."

...Click...

He calls me back and says, "Dustin, I talked with my co-leader with ICA. He wants to meet you tomorrow at the Pit, 3:30, or whatever." (The Pit is the central meeting forum area in the middle of campus for students to hang out. It is open air and is a great space to hang between classes). I said, "What?" I responded, "Why?" He said, "You're supposed to be one of our leaders. You're going to help us bring revival on the campus." I thought, "What?" He didn't even explain himself. He was so happy to get it done that he hung up on me. I'm sitting in my chair at this point thinking, "What just happened?"

Years later, Dan told me that he was literally sitting at his computer keyboard and he had just prayed. "Lord, take care of my finances, take care of my school, I give you those things and Lord I want to see revival on our campus."

Those three things he was praying for were the exact three directives I spoke about and from that point on he and Daniel knew immediately that I was called to help them lead the Forest Fire 1997 event at UNC Chapel Hill.

The next day we met at the Pit, and Daniel "G-hoon" scared me to death with this enormous vision.

12 THE PIT TALK
FALL 1996

[The best way to continue this story is only for us to have another conversation. What you are reading here is an actual recording we have transcribed about that day]

Daniel: Actually, now I remember something about that conversation. When Dan hung up with you, he called me. What I recall is, before that, we had actually been praying that the Lord would give us a sign of hope and of what to do next.

Dustin: Oh, wow. I didn't know that.

Daniel: I do remember, we were specifically praying for something more, because this was not done and we knew that Forest Fire was becoming bigger, and bigger, and bigger.

Dustin: Yeah, because Wake Forest was what? Like 500 people or something like that in attendance?

Daniel: Yeah. It was already getting bigger. Our ICA monthly meeting was becoming three to four sometimes close to five hundred. It was just those times when we were praying for GOD's sign, letting us know He's got our back, He's taking care of us and we're heading the right direction. I believe that's why Dan was so excited to get a call from Dustin.

Dustin: Because he's not excitable. He's so by the book and systematic and when I say he hung up on me, that's not like Dan Tan. He said, "What's your name, what's your number? I'll call you back." Click. I thought, "What was that?"

That's not Dan Tan. That's not how he even finishes phone calls. He's just not like that. He's not given to that kind of speed or whatever. He's more by the book. He's better at this than us.

Anyways, we met and I remember G-hoon really just shared the vision with me and he's a kind of guy that doesn't give you an out. So, I did not have a way to say, "no." So, we were together in this!

[laughter] [BOTH]

Dustin: With G-hoon, when he is hearing GOD, it's more like you're receiving a message and it's more like a lecture or a directive than a request. There was no request built in. I just realized when I walked away that there was a bigger calling of God on this and as he spoke, it just pressed in on me. I mean sometimes when we were together, the Presence of GOD was so tangible, my entire body would feel heavy and weighted. I felt a bowing of my physical body in the greatness of GOD. And sometimes my guts would be so stirred, that it felt like a mix between butterflies and a punch in my abdomen.

I knew that this was GOD's will. There was no question about it, but he didn't even leave room for there to be a question. He just said, "This is what we're doing, this is what we're going to see, and this is what you're called to do in it." I just fell right in. It just made sense inside of the Kingdom of GOD.

It didn't make sense by human standards; it just made sense in a kingdom kind of way. By this time, throughout our daily lives in Carolina, God was doing something back then, I couldn't even walk across campus without somebody accosting me and asking me about Jesus or to pray for them. I did not have to always try to share my faith. People were drawn. It was a really weird season. This happens sometimes now even as I do street ministry, but not to the degree of back then. I want that back!

Also, on campus, people started to hear about my prayer closet and were saying stuff to make jest of me like, "I heard God's in your closet." I would directly respond without flinching, "He is," and they would say, "Are you for real?" My response, "Yeah. You should come sometime." We leave the door unlocked. Just go slip in; it's the closet in the hallway that has a sign on the outside that says, "Please remove your shoes before entering…"

We used to leave the door unlocked at the "Green House." People would just come and go as they wanted. There were people saved in my closet. They would come, walk in, have access and be saved. Some folks found it by accident and GOD met them. The stories rocked!!!!!

They would turn their lives back to God and be renewed and be used by Him or whatever. God was moving and touching people in random ways in my closet. I don't even know all the stories. All I know is that my closet got really used even when I wasn't there.

There are stories about people coming in and being affected then leaving weeping. Once in a while someone would come in when no one was there. They would come out after one of my housemates had come home. My housemates would see them leave affected. It's bizarre what GOD was

61

doing. His Presence was in the closet and people knew it. They believed His Presence stayed in my closet. Some of them went home and made their own closets. HAHAHAHA!

You know what? There were a couple of times His presence came so strong in that closet, He would whisper in my ear while I was still on campus, "Hurry home, I'm there."

I remember being on Franklin Street, near Alumni Hall thinking, "I can't wait for the bus." I would literally run probably a mile and a half to two miles all the way from campus back to the Green House to be there. I remember going in throwing down my book bag, sometimes forgetting and leaving the door open (which the guys didn't like), my shoes would fly off. I'd go diving into the closet. I really honestly did this. Just diving in the Presence. Man, that's good stuff. I want that in my new prayer closet I am building right now. I have kept a prayer closet in every place I have lived since then.

It was -- insanity --. It was just that passion and His Presence was there. We did not have money, but we had HIM.

I remember sometimes doing that and then thinking I'd only prayed for a couple of minutes and getting out and it had literally been three, four or whatever hours later in the middle of night sometimes well past midnight. There's just this Presence of GOD that makes time pass and you just don't notice. It is happening some even as I write these books. It is awesome to be enraptured by HIS love. HE is so beautiful. Even as I share these things, I am stirred again for more!!!!! More of HIM!

As I entered ICA, and their activities, I learned a lot. G-hoon already shared about their habits, but could you elaborate like on how you guys met to pray, because you guys had a habit of prayer that was like, you dropped everything and met any time and it was extremely passionate and powerful. I learned about unction from ICA.

13 UNCTION IN PRAYER
BEGINNING IN 1996

(From Daniel's words and our conversation).

Daniel: I know at one of our locations, we weren't meeting regularly. Which of those locations, I cannot remember right now. At times we would just pray outside together somewhere. It didn't matter where we met so long as we met and prayed. As a group, I think there were about 12 of us that would meet on a regular basis.

We would generally call one other and meet up after lunch or around 3:00 PM in front of Davis Library or at the Pit. It was organized; we typically did not meet at random. We were intentionally in coming together just the few of us and praying.

There would be moments when the Lord would speak and call us to prayer. He generally would alert Dan or me to this. He would just speak and we'd hear His voice. This happened further along down the line once we had been praying together for some time.

I mean, I would hear the Lord one minute and the next call Dan and a couple of other guys without notice and tell them, "I need everybody now." We would meet in the next hour or two literally. Some of the women or some of the guys who were living off campus, they would come rushing in. We learned had to be sensitive to His leading and it wasn't enough to just pray when we had it scheduled.

Dustin: Even NC State.

Daniel: Ya, some of them didn't like that and it was hard. I was considered a demanding leader, but they came. They came out of obedience. One thing that they believed is that the Lord was speaking in the midst of us, and I think they were running towards that.

When we got together, it was one of those things, man. Sometimes we would just pray quietly and be still in His Presence. Back then, I don't think we used the term "Presence."

Dustin: No.

Daniel: We just knew of the LORD...

Dustin: It's just the glory. It's just the Spirit. In those moments HE just felt real, close, personal, near and big.

Daniel: Yeah. We would use the terms like, "Let's be still and know Him." Using the Bible verse.

In some other times, we would just cry out. Some of these folks, they weren't comfortable praying loud or praying with passion. I always encouraged them. I think I actually pushed them really hard to get out of their comfort zone.

We really prayed a lot and sometimes we would pray right through the day and into the night. One of them was ICA monthly meetings and praise nights. We prayed through the entire night. We actually did a lot of those overnight prayers. Our prayer meetings...

Dustin: I miss the all nighters.

Daniel: ...usually when we prayed, I think we prayed a minimum two to three hours.

Dustin: I think that's where I got my real passionate prayer-life. I grew up staunch, straight-laced Southern Baptist and you pray, "God, if it be Thy will and Thy Kingdom, and hallowed be your name," stuff. It was praying in King James English, But, these prayer meetings were real and were just straight prayer asking GOD in our modern vernacular for HIS intervention and we prayed for specifics and everyone prayed even in their own languages and sometimes over top of each other, but it never felt out of order. It always felt right.

There was just conversation about it, and even though I've been around prayer in the Vineyard at this point, it didn't affect me as much as being around that prayer and that culture of prayer, man I learned that just the aggression of angst, the aggression and the audacity of desperation and the longing and the crying out and the groaning of his spirit, both tore us, and was in us, and went through us.

I remember just throwing down and crying out for GOD's mercy. It was just really hard-core prayer times.

Daniel: I think it was in those times specifically for that season that the Lord had given me a gift of leading prayer meetings.

There was a lot of authority when I was leading with prayers. It was one of those things where in different meetings and even different settings and different conferences, and retreats, where I was not necessarily the leader I would somehow end up leading prayer.

Often times, after worship, the message and then during prayer and ministry time, I would often go up and lead the prayer meetings. The Lord just really blessed those times. What should have been a couple of songs to end-cap the meeting of that particular session, would usually go for hours and people just breaking down.

That same thing was happening in our ICA prayer meetings. I mean, we were bawling whenever we were praying because He was allowing us to pray into the campus and all the things that we were praying, I don't think there was any single person with dry eyes when we would play like that.

People were in their tears and all their, what do you call those things...

Dustin: Snot.

Daniel: Snot. Was just coming out, and we were just...

Dustin: I mean, seriously snot went onto the floor as we were face down. I'm not...

Daniel: ...we were affected.

Dustin: I'd never seen anything like that.

Daniel: We were praying...

Dustin: People walked away with raspy voices, aching and your body hurt when you're done.

Daniel: Yeah.

Dustin: I remember.

Daniel: We were on our knees.

Dustin: Yes, on our knees.

Daniel: We were on our knees, face down.

Dustin: Because you used to call out, "On your knees. Face down before God."

Daniel: That's right. I did not have it any other way.

Dustin: You had no room for any other way.

Daniel: I don't like this being comfortable, sitting down

Dustin: That's right.

Daniel: No, no, no. No chairs. We get on our knees, we put our face down. Some of the girls...

Dustin: ...and we cut the fat.

[laughter] [BOTH]

Daniel: Some of the girls actually did not like that. They were uncomfortable. They were saying that, their clothes, blah, blah, blah, their makeup. These are the seasons where I didn't care.

Dustin: You told them to wear different clothes and to wear no makeup.

Daniel: Yeah. I told them, "You put your makeup on knowing that you're coming to a prayer meeting, too bad."

That's what I used to say. I said, "Too bad. Your makeup will get messed up." They'd say, "Oh, I have a dinner meeting afterwards." I don't care. This is what's happening right now. Again, the cool thing is...

Dustin: It worked.

Daniel: ...as harsh as I was and perhaps even immature, even in that midst, they were obedient because they respected the Holy Spirit moving in that time.

Dustin: You could not deny the Presence of GOD.

Daniel: Exactly.

Dustin: You could not deny the heavy hand of GOD and that is the thing. You would do anything HE led and you didn't mind being beat up a little bit if you needed to be so that you could be who you're called to be. Actually, that's discipline and that's what disciples love.

PRAYER LEADING TO DISCIPLES

Disciples love discipline. It's proved that you're a son and a daughter. GOD doesn't discipline those He doesn't love, and so you long for it in a certain way so that you know that you get better.

When you really know you're a disciple, you can know you're a real disciple when you are in those moments where you recognize there's something that's got to change in you.

You can't quite figure out what it is, but you just wish that God will beat the snot out of you or that someone will rip you a new one and then someone prophetically speaks into you and it's the most harsh word you ever heard and you think, "Wow, isn't that like medicine to my soul."

That's when discipleship is great, when discipline becomes beloved to us. You know you are a mature disciple, then you say, "This is me. I don't need no milk. Bring it."

Daniel: That's right.

Dustin: Flesh dying in Jesus name. Bring on more of that. Make me more like Jesus. There's this real longing to shed anything of the world and to shed anything that held us back from Jesus' Presence, and that can only come because people have interacted with His Presence in the first place and can't imagine being without it anymore. The love of God enacted on us being so overwhelming that we cannot have it any longer.

Daniel: Yeah, absolutely. Wow, just going back to the...

Dustin: That's the power of getting into this. You feel it.

Daniel: ...The phrase "cut the fat."

Daniel: Anyway, we must be soldiers, basically the best of the best. Well-trained soldiers. One thing that I knew is we needed a team of people who were willing to die for God. You know...

Dustin: You actually used to talk about that. And then we die for each other. We get each other's back at all costs, but we would die for God. We're willing to die for God.

Daniel: Literally...

Dustin: You used to say that.

Daniel: Yeah. Again, it may sound very stupid, or immature, and idiotic now, but at that time, we were seriously at a point of willingness to die, if that's what it takes, to bring revival to our campus. We were willing to lay our life down.

Dustin: We just didn't care. We cared more about Him and each other than we cared about ourselves.

Daniel: Cut the fat comes from that kind of mindset. Like, "Your make up will be ruined, I don't care," if you're more worried about your makeup than revival, then that's fat. I was building a team of just lean and just ready to go to war at any given notice, and the skills were so sharpened that they could not only take care of themselves, but take care of each other.

We were fighting and we were fighters, especially through prayer. I remember this now, a lot, now that we're talking. Some of the things that were happening individually were this, and I believed this is why when we got together as a team, our prayer was powerful.

Individually, we were worshiping God. We were doing our quiet time and were disciplined. We were reading the scripture, we were praying deeply with the scripture, and we were very faithful to the Lord, and we were listening to Him.

NO BATHROOM BREAK...

Not only that, this was a season when the Lord was blessing us with the Holy Spirit, and the way He was doing that, manifested like this.

A couple of brothers would come to where I was living and we took out our guitars and our song book and we'd start playing. We would get so into it that we would just literally praise for three, four hours, and not that the amount matters, but you know what, I cannot remember the last time anybody told me that they were just sitting there with another person, just praising, in their room for four hours straight.

No bathroom break, no nothing. We were just completely captured by the Holy Spirit.

It was one of those things where we weren't even looking at each other. We had our eyes closed, and were just singing, and praising with our guitars and we all knew exactly what we were singing.

From the verse to the second to the chorus, coming back to the chorus. It was just weird.

Dustin: One voice, one mind, one heart kind of thing.

Daniel: I mean this spirit was moving, connecting us. We were like truly connected because we were living that kind of a community life. When we came together as a bonding, the 12 of us; I forgot how many exactly, maybe 16. It makes sense that the prayer time just elevates to the 100 percent intensity right away.

We never had to work it up. Right Dustin? It wasn't one of those things "OK, here's the reason why we're here, we are going to pray for this, this, this, this, this."

Dustin: You are already up. You didn't have to dial up because you were always dialed in!

Daniel: Yeah, we would just get on our knees and pray, and boom, people started praying. We started hearing loud noises, crying.

It wasn't just one of those...actually, there were even set prayer sessions when we came in, and everyone is waiting for the direction, and I would say nothing. I would say "let's pray," and we just started praying. Because I knew I didn't have to say anything, the Holy Spirit would take care of that.

Dustin: There's travail too. Just people travailing. Just struggling, travail. I remember just the groanings in your guts. People felt other people's pains and they interceded for them as if their own life depended on it. When intersession would kick in it was full force groanings, the achings, the longing. I am actually experiencing the groaning here in the last little bit as we discuss this and I haven't experienced those in 15 years, since then really. It's coming back. I want to frame it just a little bit more too. I know I didn't mention it yet, I want to mention it here.

14 THE FAB FOUR
FALL 1996

We were already traveling and seeing God move at different churches and stuff. Anyway, God was moving on their campuses. And then, here we are, heading into Forest Fire. We started to do these prayer meetings that were specifically for Forest Fire. It was me, G-hoon, Dan Tan, and Jeff Linn. The four of us would get together.

This was beyond all the other prayer meetings. I mean, we prayed for everything. But this was a prayer meeting just for leadership and planning for Forest Fire. We were getting together every week. It would be more than once a week, oftentimes, but it was at least once a week that we got together. And we planned. And this was on top of all the other prayer calls that G-hoon gave us throughout the week.

Starting in the fall of 1996, we were praying for God to move in February of 1997. We chose February 15th, which was a ridiculous date, being that it was the weekend of Valentine's Day. I don't even really know why we chose that date, because it did not work.

We reserved the Pit so that we could have what we called, "Christ Awareness Week." The whole week long we had the Pit reserved and we had ministries put out tables, we did worship in the Pit, people took turns doing outreach as well as some of us would preach, which took some doing because of Valentine's Day. We actually had the Pit reserved through Valentine's Day which made some people mad because they couldn't do Valentine's Day stuff or sell stuff, or even be all Valentine's-y about the fraternities and sororities.

We blocked it. We didn't mean to, but we were there. So Valentine's, it was all about Jesus's love for the campus [laughs] .

So, anyways, we had Christ Awareness Week that was scheduled for that week before the 15th, and then Saturday, the 15th, would be the big event.

The main Forest Fire 1997 event would include worship, a testimony by Robert Brickey, a former Duke basketball player, a testimony by Coach Sylvia Hatchell, the women's basketball coach, through a relationship that I had from way back in the beginning of this story. And then it would be some fun "Saturday Night Live" kind of intro, welcome.

There would be some, I think, more kicking worship music to bring us into the service or some of the sermon, and then there was teaching by Clayton King, who preached and amazing sermon. Then at the very end of all of that, there were concerts back to back with two local bands.

God had stirred us up for this big event planned on Saturday, and it was really spoken to us that we're supposed to expand it. In prior years, it had been like 500 people on attendance, so it was normal to expect growth. We already saw that we could get as much as 800 to 1,000 people.

In one of our first meetings, I remember praying, and G-hoon had been the "cut-the-fat guy" and "in-our-face guy," and I had been this "crazy vision guy." I remember sitting down and saying, "We got to believe for more. God says, 'Get a basketball court, or go bigger.' We can't just do Carroll Hall. We need bigger, bigger, bigger."

It's not the University that concerns us. This is what concerns us:

"For we are not contending against flesh and blood, but against the principalities, against the powers, against the world rulers of this present darkness..." (Ephesians 6:12, Revised Standard Version)

God's message is clear: His work must go on! And the battle is the Lord's, because only He can lead us into sure victory. Now is the time for us to be on our knees, because The Adversary is working overtime while we delay.

Grace and peace be with you all dear brothers and sisters. May God show this place how awesome He is. Remember-- one week...

Forest Fire 1997 Coordinators on their knees... and in the grip of His Grace...

Dan Tan   dantan@email.unc.edu
Dustin Hedrick DSHedrick@aol.com
G-hoon Kim   ghoonkim@email.unc.edu
Jeff Lin jlin7@aol.com

I can't remember what our initial place was going to be that we got. We got one of them locked down as a fallback, and then we started going after the basketball gym. They told us, to get the basketball gym, there had to be a lot of things for that play out.

Number one, you've got to get the basketball team to say that they won't have practice and that they'll let us have the gym that weekend. Which was not going to happen. It's February.

February's before March. If you're from UNC-Chapel Hill, you know March is madness. That's all it is. There is nothing else going on at UNC-Chapel Hill except for basketball in February and March.

So I was supposed to go in to Coach Sylvia Hatchell and ask her, "Hey, do you mind not having practice? Or making sure the women are off the court so we can have your facility? Will you sign off on this so we can have it, and have the facility on a Saturday before you guys go into March Madness?" I did. And actually, that also included her making sure that there's no game on our day.

So I walked in with just the audacity of Jesus, after having spoken to the crowd at the Easter service, and I said, "Coach Hatchell, we just ask if you'd let us have the gym." She's says, "I know you. You're our preacher." I was said, "Yes, ma'am." Because I'd been going to the games all those years and spoken back in their national championship win in 1994.

And she says, "So you want my gym." I was responded, "Just for a little while, ma'am. Just one night." And she says, "Why?" When I told her why, she turned to me and she said, "Of course you can have my gym." She said, "I love your heart. I am for this. I am for GOD moving on this campus and in young people. You tell me what else I can do for you, and I'm there."

I said, "Would you mind opening the meeting by speaking a welcome to the crowd?" And she's said, "All right. I can do that, too." So we already had Coach Sylvia Hatchell's cover and her blessing. It was amazing. She's just an amazing lady. I mean, the woman is awesome. It was like the best thing ever.

FOR IMMEDIATE RELEASE: January 21, 1997
CONTACT: Dustin Hedrick, ▅▅▅▅▅▅▅▅▅
            Dan Tan, ▅▅▅▅▅▅▅▅▅
            email: FFire97@aol.com

FOREST FIRE COMES TO UNC'S CARMICHAEL AUDITORIUM, FEB. 15 AT 7 PM.

Over 5000 college students will converge on the campus of The
University of North Carolina at Chapel Hill for the second annual
Forest Fire Conference on Saturday, February 15 at 7 p.m..

The Forest Fire Conference was started in 1996 at Wake Forest
University, where a few students caught a vision of promoting unity
among Christian students for the sake of a greater witness, personal
renewal and spreading the gospel. The result was a conference that had
over 600 students attending from over 16 different schools, from all
over the United States, including Virginia, Louisiana and California.
Over 40 students came forward and responded to the call to either
accept Christ as their savior or to renew their commitment to Christ.

Although Forest Fire is targeted to undergraduate and graduate
students, the conference is also open to the general public.

The speaker for this year's conference is Clayton King. He was also
the speaker for the first Forest Fire Conference. Clayton graduated
from Gardner-Webb University with a degree in ministry and is a
ordained minister with the Southern Baptist Association. He is the
coordinator of Crossroads Youth Camp at Gardner-Webb University and
also coordinates Jacob's Well, a Christian music festival at Gardner-
Webb. Clayton has gone on short-term missions to Kenya, Rwanda,
Russia, Romania, Hungary, Jamaica, India and Canada. He currently
gives motivational talks at public schools, concerning teens issues
such as sex, teen pregnancy, drugs and alcohol. He also tours with
his band, Monogamous Fish. Clayton lives in Shelby, NC.

Former Duke University basketball star, Robert Brickey, and UNC
Women's Basketball Coach, Sylvia Hatchell, will also speak at Forest
Fire.

Robert Brickey is currently on staff with Young Life Ministries in
Durham, working with high school students at Hillside High School in
Durham, NC. He has also started a non-profit group, Community Impact,
to help underprivileged children in his hometown of Fayetteville.
Robert was a three-year starter on the Duke University basketball team
from 1987 to 1990.

Copy : Forest Fire 1997 Press Release

We came back and told the property manager for the building, for Carmichael, who was really not supportive of our vision, that we had gotten Coach Sylvia Hatchell's approval, which he could not believe. Then he went on to say, "Well, you can't have the building because they're going to work on the floors and there are many other issues as well."

Whenever they said they were going to work on the floors, they said they would take a certain amount of time and there's no way that we would have it for weeks in that time frame. Again, I don't know why we chose February. We just felt like it was necessary. We couldn't choose March for that place, but we could have probably chosen April or May, but God said February, we did February.

So we went to prayer. At each point, whenever we got pushed back, we went to prayer. We prayed for Coach Sylvia Hatchell's heart, but she was already with us. She was awesome. We started praying for this because we knew it was harder. We knew the building was nixed, so we started praying. We got together and we prayed that night.

We prayed and we prayed and we prayed. We prayed until we came to a point where somebody there prayed, "GOD, don't let that man go to sleep until he calls us and says that he'll help us. Let him know that he may never sleep again. Keep him awake, Jesus, until he helps us."

Forest Fire 1997

Yesterday, January 13th, the Forest Fire planners found out that former
Duke basketball star Robert Brickey and UNC Women's Basketball coach
Sylvia Hatchell will both be giving testimonies at Forest Fire.

Attendance is expected at over 5000 on February 15th.
Over twenty schools are expected. Clayton King has been the confirmed
speaker for months.

Volunteers for counselors or other needs have come from every major
evangelical fellowship at UNC-CH. The Billy Graham Training Center will
be training counselors. Counselor training will start in two weeks. Big
Wednesday and Mark Williams are fired up for the free post-Forest Fire
concert later on that night. Promo flyers are ready to flood the
campuses. Press releases are ready to go out to every major regional
newspaper in North Carolina and several major nation-wide Christian
publications. WRTP 1530 AM is ready to do public service announcements
interviews, or promos for Forest Fire.

Today, we received a phone call that our request to use Carmichael
Auditorium, where the women's basketball team plays...

... was denied.

The athletic department cleared it, and Coach Hatchell cleared it as
well, but a department at UNC-CH that approves "major events" denied
use of the facility. This places everything on hold until certain
obstacles can be removed. Approved facility usage is one thing that
University "major event" approval is contigent upon, so even though
press releases, color posters, and radio promos are waiting for the
green light, legally, we cannot promote the event. Promotion of the
event cannot occur until the facility is cleared for use and the event
is confirmed by the University. The official making this decision made
his decision within his understanding of certain "unknowns" that might
affect Forest Fire.

There are four major items that NEED MAJOR PRAYER.

One is the potential of a fire hazard. Men's lacrosse is playing a
scrimmage that day, and usually the lane running around the Auditorium is
blocked off for usage by concessions and other personnel. It is also a
fire lane that leads directly to the Auditorium floor, and if it is
blocked, then getting truckloads of equipment onto the basketball floor
would not be possible until after the game, by which time it would be too
late to set up. There is also a possibility that the fire marshall would
not approve of a big event in the Auditorium if access to the fire lane
was restricted. There is also construction going on behind Carmichael,
near the fire lane and also near the only loading area that leads onto the
Auditorium floor.

All these factors need to be either removed or changed enough so as not
to be a problem with the fire marshall or for set-up crews.

The next day, the guy calls Dan Tan and says, "All right. I'm going to help you guys. Not because I want to, but because I knew if I don't help you all, I'll probably never sleep again. I couldn't sleep." Dan comes back and tells us, "You won't believe what happened." We didn't. It was amazing.

So we got it approved that we could still work out a deal to get it. But

The second is the women's basketball team. Morning practice will have to end early enough to allow time for the University services to set up flooring on the gym floor and setup the stage, and for the sound technician to rig everything up. That was also a concern of the official, that there would not be enough time to setup before the event.

The third, and perhaps most crucial item for the University, is for funding. Rental of the Auditorium, floor covering and stage set-up, on-site off-duty University Police, University technicians and other workers push the total fee to be paid to the University to an estimated $4500. The University has stated that they "need to see money in our account," before they can approve the facility. There are currently church boards who have decided to support Forest Fire but who are still deciding upon the amount. Pray that they decide soon and move quickly, and pray that more support comes in from others who are led to share for Forest Fire.

ICA has never received funding from the University, and is not a ministry that keeps on-hand a budget of the size required for Forest Fire. The University then, is probably concerned that payment will be a problem, since they are not aware of the full extent of our fund-raising.

The fourth item, and most crucial for Forest Fire 97, is that every obstacle be removed WITHIN A WEEK. If the University is to re-consider approving the event, then everything must be in place within a week or they will not allow it to go through due to the small time frame they will have to prepare their facilities.

EVERYTHING MUST BE CLEARED WITHIN A WEEK, and it needs a DIVINE MIRACLE to pull all the pieces together. On our own, we will tackle every avenue that opens up, but only GOD with a capital "G" could coordinate all the details to come together within one week.

Are you prepared to pray for a miracle? I am, because there is not a single day in my life that I am more sure of than FEBRUARY 15th for Forest Fire. If you all knew the "minor" miracles God has pulled off to bring everything into place, you would literally be blown away. We have seen God answer prayer after prayer after prayer, and -- well, I don't have time to write all that He has done, but __ PLEASE PRAY. __ And get more people to pray. And pray hard, like you've never prayed before.

Thanks, bros and sis's. We ask you not to pray for the sake of Forest Fire, or for the sake of this year's hosts--
we ask of you that you pray for the sake of the Gospel of Jesus Christ. And for no other reason, because this is HIS event, this is HIS day, and all the praise and glory belongs ONLY to HIM.

May your faith be stretched so far beyond what you can ever imagine, as God proves His faithfulness and defends HIS WORK. Pray with fervor, cry out to God in desperation, and know that HE HEARS THE VOICES OF HIS CHILDREN CRYING OUT IN THE WILDERNESS, and HE HAS COMPASSION ON THEM. And He will PROVE faithful, because that is His promise.

there was still the question of when the guys would come and finish the floors. So we prayed and we prayed and we prayed. We got contacted back. Something happened with another deal they were doing. They were held over longer or something. I think they were doing floors at NC State or something, and they couldn't come at the time they were going to, and they pushed UNC's date back.

What that meant was that not only could they not remove the floors when they said they would, but that meant that we didn't have to worry about brand new floors. We had been quoted in our contract an extra $5,000 to rent the space just to have the floors covered and have chairs put down.

They told us, when he came back to us and said that they couldn't have the floors done beforehand, the property manager says, "This is working out. You guys are lucky or whatever. Not only can we not get the floors done, but we're not going to charge you for the fee to cover the floors because we're not going to worry about them because we have to take them up anyways."

So, guys, we got that place and GOD answered at each point. We got Sylvia Hatchell's approval and blessing. We got that guy to work with us, he got the date changed for the floors to be redone, and he dropped the cost because when it was changed, it made it so that we didn't have to worry about the floors at all.

Not only that, but everything we prayed for, I can't remember all the other things we prayed for, whether it was people being able to speak or things being able to happen. Every single thing fell into place, finally started coming in. Details started happening. Some other things we prayed for were coverage by the media that was helpful that would give more people information in our area before it happened and we ended up in the newspapers and on TV! Every time we turned around, something came through. Finances came through as well as people gave money to support the work. How would a bunch of college students get $15,000? I mean that is like $30,000 now.

FOREST

FIRE 97

ESTIMATED BUDGET

AUDITORIUM FEES (Includes rental, staging setup, flooring, labor, technicians, staff, housekeeping, UNC Security Services, Emergency Medical Services)	$10070
SOUND SYSTEM (Includes sound engineer, set-up of equipment, and on-site operation)	$1000
COUNSELOR TRAINING MATERIALS (for 200 counselors)	$1500
COUNSELOR BIBLES (to be given out by counselors as needed)	$1000
PRINTING (Brochures, flyers, posters, response cards, misc. materials)	$1200
EVENT T-SHIRTS	$3000
PROJECTION EQUIPMENT (Two high intensity projectors and two large screens)	$600
FOOD	$500
SPEAKER HONORARIUMS	$250
MISC. EXPENSES (On-site communications, first-aid station, speaker lodging, misc. supplies)	$500
TOTAL	$19620.00

Revised January 19, 1997

Date: Tue, Feb 4, 1997 3:25 PM EDT
From: JLin7
Subj: extended story in Chapel Hill Herald
To: ████████████████, DSHedrick, ████████████████

The Durham Herald-Sun
Sunday, February 2, 1997

Organizers Hope To Attract 10,000 to Christian Gathering
By Susan Broili

CHAPEL HILL - Organizers hope up to 10,000 Christian college students
will converge on UNC for the second annual Forest Fire Conference this
month.

Sylvia Hatchell, womenís basketball coach at the University of North
Carolina at Chapel Hill, will open the Feb. 15 conference in Carmichael
Auditorium at 7 p.m. The conference also features former Duke University
basketball player Robert Brickey and Baptist minister Clayton.

UNC senior Dustin Hedrick, conference coordinator, said the name has
nothing to do with putting out forest fires, but rather with starting a fire
- metaphorically speaking.

The conference originated last year at Wake Forest University in
Winston-Salem and drew 600 students.

"They wanted the fire to start at Wake Forest - a fire as far as the
Christian community pulling together and letting the world know. Not only
in race and denomination, but in spirit, weíre together as a body for the
purpose of praising God," Hedrick said, his voice hoarse from preaching at
a Charlotte youth revival during the weekend.

Hatchell said she readily agreed to appear at the conference.

"I support what theyíre doing. Anytime I can participate in anything that
will enrich the lives of the students and direct them in a positive,

Christian way, Iíll do it," Hatchell said.

Hatchell said she thinks it helps being a Christian coach.

"You build a lot of character. You always have an inspiration type thing for yourself of the kids," Hatchell said.

The Tar Heel women pray before and after each game.

"And not necessarily to win," Hatchell said. "I pray that no one gets hurt, that I, as a coach, will have the knowledge to do a good jobÖ that we play hard, play smart and play together."

Hatchell, coach at UNC since 1986, said her players decided to pray after games, with players taking turns saying prayers of "thanksgiving - whether we win or lose, to keep us unified and healthy."

The next time theyíll be praying and playing will be at 2 p.m. today when they meet Wake Forest in Winston-Salem.

The team is ranked sixth nationally, with a record of 18-1, and ranked first in the ACC, with a record of 9-0. Hatchellís 1993-4 team won the NCAA womenís basketball championship, and she was named the National Coach of the Year by USA Today and College Sports Magazine.

Hatchell and Hedrick spoke of the approximately 30 strong Christian groups on campus, including Athletes in Action and the Fellowship of Christian Athletes, and said they expect many members at the conference. Hedrick attributed the high number of group participants to a growing Christian movement among young people.

"I think our generation is realizing that God is real and we are really seeing Jesus Christ as our Lord and Savior," Hedrick said.

The Statesville native, who said he grew up in the Southern Baptist Church and was called to preach about three years ago, said young Christians are working to right wrongs in society.

"Thereís a lot of things in society that could use help - anything from murder, rape, incest. Thereís a lot of anger and violence," The Christian community finally sees that they are the hope for the nation, the Lord Jesus Christ is the hope for the nation," Hedrick said.

"I just hope I see more happiness on campus and more people caring about each other and reaching out and helping each other," he added. "I'd just like to see more people my age reach out to the younger generation."

Hedrick said campus Christian groups are active in the community.

New Vision Church, a campus interdenominational church begun working about a a year ago, is working with at-rick children, while the Intervarsity Christian Fellowship is working on race relations, Hedrick said.

The conference, sponsored by family radio station WRTP AM 1530, is free, but a collection will be taken to defray the $20,000 cost, Hedrick said. Thought the conference is targeting students, the general public may also attend.

The event will last until midnight and include concerts by Big Wednesday and Mark Williams. Eugene Lee and the In Christ Alone Praise Band will lead worship and Knights for Christ, a drama group based in Stony Point, will perform "Arise, My Love."

If we needed a down payment for a certain amount on the place, we prayed and the finances would come in so that we could get the place reserved. We didn't have the whole amount initially, it was too much for us.

I think it started at $15,000 went down to $13,000 which is a lot for college students, it is beyond what we could believe for. I never raised $500, let alone $15,000. So we were praying God will give us a down payment and the money would come.

We started calling churches that we believe would get involved. It was amazing as we heard pastors say, "No," they did not want to be involved with our campus and they did not believe we were following Jesus. It was insanity. Afterward churches opened up all over the place and wanted us to come in to preach, so we did not hold unforgiveness against them. Even ones that did not support us, we would still later go and freely minister in them.

15 SPREADING THE FIRE
WINTER 1996 TO EARLY 1997

The newspapers came and wanted to interview us, from "The Daily Tar Heel" to the, "The Chapel Herald," or whatever it was called. The actual big newspaper interviewed us. We were even written about in "Decision" magazine when it was all said and done, Billy Graham's magazine. It affected our area in a massive way and it spread afterwards.

We couldn't get the support we wanted. I remember one pastor hung up on me. I thought, "Wow, that's awesome." He said, "We don't believe in what you are doing." I said, "Reaching students for Jesus? OK." I remember thinking, "Right, I guess it is not going to work out to go to that church."

We just kept going after it. Long story short, we kept going after it, we kept pressing in and then we really started to press into spreading into other campuses.

Dustin: Daniel, I don't know if you remember, this is where my memory it not great, but we started going to other campuses. I think we went to State, or Duke, or other ones.

We went as being part of their ministry or something. Being available, or maybe we were supporting them in what they were doing. Maybe you guys did worship sets or something.

There was some kind of overlap, I can't remember what it was that allowed us to connect. We started praying into this before Forest Fire. Connecting others into the campus.

I know we had contacts that stated that they were coming to our prayer meetings but there was overlap. I can't remember how it happened but there was overlap before Forest Fire.

(SIDENOTE: See the emails at the end as well as the images of the emails embedded for more of that unwritten story from the actual emails and communications, themselves. This whole thing went viral before viral was viral).

Daniel: I don't remember either.

Dustin: I don't either.

Daniel: But I do remember the ICA Praise Band used to go to other...

Dustin: Venues.

Daniel: ...venues.

Dustin: I can't remember what it was.

Daniel: We kept getting invited.

Dustin: It started to open up doors for other people that were outside of Carolina to get involved. I remember something happened in there. I just don't remember everything. Then the other thing that happened is it was the early days of technology and IT, me being a little bit of a hacker that I was; I had already been in trouble with my uncle because I had got into the backside of the CIA website, (I became notorious for this back in the day. I call it accidental hacking). Nothing was locked, and nothing had passwords, and I was not breaking the law.

I didn't even know what I did. I just figured out that you could type in the root of a domain and then if you figured out where the papers lived, you could go to the root of that area and it would list the content of the file folder.

You could see the whole tree of information. You could pick what pages you want to go to and really get into stuff.

When I went to the CIA website, I found what became later the CIA fact book, which is a public thing now, but back then I had gotten into the actual depth of site of root on the early pre-graphic web.

I just was learning about other countries. I was praying for other countries. I didn't know it was wrong. I was trying to pray for other countries. It was honest. I wanted to do intercession.

I thought to myself, "Hey, if it worked with that, it could work with other things." I routed around in campuses. I would go to a college campus website and root down in it and find the entire student directories.

I found Iowa State, Ohio State, NC State. I went through lots of colleges and pulled their root directory. I was able to get the entire student email list from these websites, it was available.

There was no password protection. They didn't know about that back then. There was no encryption. There weren't even any real laws back then on that kind of thing. I would never do this now.

But back then I ripped entire colleges 20,000, 15,000, 30,000 emails. There was also no restriction on the amount of emails you could send from an AOL account back in the day. However, if something hung up, I would type a whole boatload of email addresses in and "send."

We would send out these emails just stirring up campuses talking about what GOD was doing day -by-day. How they were stirring up groups.

We were talking about campus ministry were getting involved and praying. How they were coming into ICA and worshiping together. What was leading them to Forest Fire inviting people to come to Forest Fire.

We had responses back from around the planet. I mean around the planet. We were getting responses from campuses as far as University of Hawaii, Ohio State and Iowa State, California and all over.

We ended up getting hold of about 23 to 25 different campuses email list. We were massively emailing. Not only was it stirring people up through what GOD was doing in Carolina. Again, there was no law on spamming back then. We didn't even know what spam was.

They were being stirred up at their campuses and sharing back what GOD was doing. Even doing similar things, we were even inciting them to start prayer movements, worship movements and unity movements.

There was something stirring up on other campuses and those stories started to come back. We have got a lot of those that I have got printed off from years ago. Some of them I have lost but I have got a lot of emails of what came of Forest Fire in those days. So heading into the event...

Daniel: Actually...

Dustin: Go ahead.

Daniel: When this gets transcribed. I actually want to pause here for a second because I think we need to go back on one point you had made. It is regarding the closet. It just dawned on me. I want to draw this to a point that an understanding that I just got, just now, as we were recording this.

FOREST ▓▓▓▓▓▓▓▓▓▓▓▓▓

January 19, 1997

▓▓▓▓▓▓▓▓▓

FIRE 97

Over 5000 college students are expected to converge on the campus of The University of North Carolina at Chapel Hill for the second annual Forest Fire Conference on Saturday, February 15th at 7:00pm in Carmichael Auditorium.

Forest Fire was started in 1996 at Wake Forest University, by a handful of students with a vision of promoting unity among Christians for the sake of a greater witness, personal renewal, and evangelism. Students from over a dozen colleges attended, and around 40 students came forward that night to either accept Christ as their Savior or to renew their commitment to Christ.

The planners for Forest Fire 1996 selected In Christ Alone (ICA) Ministries to be the host for this year's Forest Fire at the University North Carolina at Chapel Hill. An additional emphasis for this year's conference is revival. The desire for unity for the sake of the Gospel and revival on campuses is also shared by Christians from other surrounding North Carolina colleges.

We would greatly appreciate any monetary support you may be prayerfully led to invest. Our budget currently stands at approximately $20,000 that will cover rental/setup fees for the auditorium, food, an honorarium, counselor training materials, publicity, and other costs. An estimated budget has been included in this letter. Underwriters of this event can have seating reserved in the front rows if requested. Other churches, ministries, and businesses are also being contacted about this event, and we are looking forward to the fruits of God's work that will be evident from this event.

Please call Dustin Hedrick or one of the other listed individuals to let us know of your decision as soon as possible. If you would like for someone to provide more details to you or to your church, please contact one of the listed individuals. Thank you, and may God bless as He has promised! We look forward to hearing from you soon.

Sincerely,

[signature]

In Christ Alone Ministries
Forest Fire 1997 Host
Ministry

(919) 929-9413
(919) 932-3045
PO Box 1232
Carrboro, NC
27510

FFire97@aol.com
http://users.aol.com/ffire97

DUSTIN HEDRICK   EVENT COORDINATOR   919-932-3045
DAN TAN   COUNSELORS/VOLUNTEERS   919-929-9413
G-HOON KIM   PRAYER /FINANCES
JEFF LIN   PUBLIC RELATIONS

Sponsored by
In Christ Alone
Ministries

16 BACK TO THE CLOSET
AN ASIDE ON THE YEARS 1995-1997 AT THE GREEN HOUSE

Daniel: When Dustin was talking about his closet where God was, at that Green House. First of all, it is a Green House not as in place you grow vegetables but as in the house was green, painted green. First of all, the closet really existed. Second of all, the closet really had GOD in there.

Some of you who are very theologically attuned, you may say, "how can you contain GOD." This is not what this is about. I mean, GOD, for whatever reason, chose to exist inside that closet in a way that was not like outside of it.

Dustin: Bizarre.

Daniel: The Presence was inside. I remember going inside that closet. Let me describe this closet. It was not one of those big closets as in a bedroom closet. It was one of those coat closets like you would see in an older home. So the coat closet was not like a two feet by six or seven feet like you'd see today. This was more like three by three or four by four.

It was really small; it was one of those closets where all you could do is go in there if you sat with your leg crossed, that's about it. Dustin painted the place in dark blue. He put about two feet high of cushions so once you go inside and close the door, you're basically in this little capsule.

It's dark, it's comfortable, and there was music going on with the speakers hanging from the top. The best way I can describe it is from a movie a long time ago called "Stargate."

In the movie "Stargate," this is a sci-fi movie, some spaceship comes down to the pyramid. The way somebody gets out of the spaceship onto the ground; there are these rings that come and they get beamed down.

That closet was that beamed capsule. That is exactly what it felt like. You go inside and boom, you get transported, you get beamed up to the heaven. It is exactly what it felt like.

Then when you are done with your prayer. You get beamed right back down. It was like an elevator to heaven. [laughs] Literally a direct elevator.

The reason why I bring this up now is to show God's Presence was there, it was HIS resting place. Why this is so important plays into the succession, the cadence, the rhythm of how it all happened.

You didn't know why, we didn't know either, you just somehow got pulled. You were driven to have this place set aside for HIS glory.

WATCH THIS CLIP ON THE PRAYER CLOSET AND DUSTIN SHARES STORIES ABOUT HOW GOD WOULD MEET PEOPLE IN THE CLOSET AND THE PRESENCE

Dustin: There's just nothing else. I could not even think of anything else, but HIS glory.

Daniel: Yes and you found the place where HIS glory would come. It came and then the Lord led you to a place, to the people who are hungry and seeking.

Then out of that comes a deep just passionate, accessions of prayer and the prayer building up to the actual climax event, just all out worship. Think about the prayer house.

Dustin: I know, I didn't even think of that. I used to go in that closet and then GOD would send me out with special adventures in joining HIM and sharing specific words HE wanted to share with people. I would go straight out of the closet on a directive and find the person, say the thing GOD led and they would accept Jesus. It was easy. It was outflow. Heaven had come to earth and GOD was going after people. The Good Shepherd is always seeking and saving!

And in that same vein, I started the prayer house in Kensington as well as am beginning a new one in the North of Washington, DC.

Daniel: That's the first thing that we did.

Dustin: You're right. We started a place for prayer, The Prayer House in Kensington and it is happening again!

Daniel: Then GOD came.

Dustin: I would have never thought of that.

WATCH THIS CLIP FROM THE GAS STATION AT THE END OF THE ROAD WHERE ONE OF THE FIRST HAPPENINGS OUT OF THE PRAYER CLOSET TOOK PLACE

17 FOREST FIRE | THE BIG DAY
FEBRUARY 14-15, 1997

Daniel: Anyway, so leading to the event, I only pushed this forward because I'm aware of us running out of recording and I want to make sure we don't lose this. Leading into the event, it was an interesting thing that all of these campuses started getting stirred up.

Dustin: The day of the event, I remember thinking that no one was coming. I just had this moment. I thought, "Nobody is going to come, it's Valentine's weekend, we're idiots."

I was just praying and I was nervous, at the same time. I know that's the wrong way to be, but hey, I was a college kid and I didn't know the right way to be towards God. It would have been good if just GOD was there. I know the right answers.

This is the same college kid who got excited because I actually got the chance to touch the floors and rub the floor at the exact place where Michael Jordan took his last step before he dunked on NC State, the first dunk in a Carolina ball game.

I'm just saying this is the kind of kid I was back then. I was nervous. I thought, "Oh my goodness. Nobody is coming, and we had prepared and we worked so hard. We were just in prayer and seeking the LORD," and everyone came. People came and they came from all over our state.

It was so surprising. We didn't know. We had no tickets, we had no responses. We didn't know, but people came. Oh we had some responses, but it wasn't like this.

People came from other states, other campuses, all the campus ministries that you can imagine showed up. We had, I think, it was 23 or 24 college campuses represented, which is shocking. 24 college campuses represented, it's something a bunch of college kids pulled off. I think that' just shocking.

Then we had campuses from all over, multiple states. People had come in from different states to be there. I mean, we had the random who drove in from New York and just crazy stuff like that, and that's just a couple of folks, we had people from all these other states like SC, GA, VA, TN, and all the local states as well.

It was shocking to me. That's so many states involved. So many campuses involved.

That night GOD just built up. Sometimes the sound didn't work right and the projector didn't work right, the technology was iffy, but God's Presence was there, Clayton nailed the sermon. He nailed it. The worship team was on. It was insanity.

Both Robert Brickey & Sylvia Hatchel brought it, just such precious words as spoken to who we are, and even the band's efforts were really a blessing. It was like an end-cap, like icing on the cake because the real ministry, it seemed like, was really kicking and done when Clayton brought it home.

We saw 250 people make decisions, not for salvation. Two hundred and fifty people made decisions for ministry and missions. Two hundred and fifty people went into ministry or missions, not salvation. Salvation was a total other amount. I don't know. All I know is a 250 that came forward from ministry and missions.

It was shocking what GOD did, and then after that call, Clayton just opened for salvations and people came and there were lines. There were just people everywhere down on the floor, when he finished, before the bands played.

(Later, after the initial writing of this book and these recordings, Daniel found some footage from backstage that his brother had taken on an old camera and we just converted it. It shows some of the event as well as people making decisions for Christ. It is amazing because there were hundreds if not a thousand students making decisions for Jesus outside while we kept on ministering, that's why the stands emptied just after Clayton spoke and before the closing worship and we never knew what happened).

We didn't get to see all that played out because we were too busy leading. It was unbelievable what GOD did. That wasn't the most exciting part. We had thousands. How many were there? Thousands.

Daniel: Thousands, yes.

Dustin: Thousands all up in this basketball stadium. We were shocked. It was just thousands and thousands of students.

Anyway, the thing that was exciting was the outflow. Starting that very night, we were leaving that place and people were being affected, people were ministering to each other, people were leading other people to Jesus outside the building, people were leaving and telling others about the Lord directly. They couldn't help it.

The same night, people were calling people and repenting, and reconnecting, and leading their friends and family to Jesus. People were so affected they moved immediately.

Even though it was late, they moved immediately to present the gospel. Other people, they emailed back telling us what movement started on their campus that very week because they went back and said they wanted it too. Some of them invited to come speak, and to do ministry.

We got emails back from people that heard radio stations where people had testified the next Monday and they had both been at the conference.

One had been at the conference that had testified at the radio station and the other had listened to the radio station and thought, "Oh my goodness, there's somebody else from the conference." As far away as Charlotte, North Carolina on the country radio station during the mornings, a lot of people had to go to work and they heard it on the morning radio show that morning as they were heading to start their day.

WATCH A CLIP WHERE DUSTIN SHARES MORE ON THIS OUTSIDE CARMICHAEL ARENA

We heard about just so much happening on campuses and at schools. Our story started spreading across campuses. We didn't even make it to all the campuses that were affected.

Other campuses started having unity meetings, worship meetings, praise meetings, prayer meetings, and they kept calling us and talking with us, and emailing us and saying, "What should we do next?" We encouraged them. And we were a bunch of kids that didn't know.

We started going into fasting and prayer immediately. We got called in to minister across the state.

We were traveling as far as Appalachian State University all the way to ECU, Wake Forest, were seeing God moving on campuses such as UNC Charlotte and churches where God was moving. And it literally catapulted us in the ministry. As a matter of fact, I was catapulted in this revival ministry until about 1998. And I was ordained into preaching ministry in 1997 before I even went to seminary due to the sheer activity of GOD. There was no stopping it. (There are so many stories I cannot add here that came from that era. They will be in my other book).

Even my youth from Temple Baptist, Todd Payne pulled off a big event with 600 students coming out at Alexander Central High School because of what they're passionate about from seeing it at Forest Fire. A group of us were invited to go through the school and share our faith as well as give hope to these students due to Todd's opening the door. Todd is now a worker in missions work and meeting Clayton through this event helped to catapult him as well.

People started saying, "I saw it. I can do it too," and they did it. Even when we'd start preaching in churches and so extended protracted meetings, and some churches had meetings every single night.

There was so much that stirred up. God did so much, and we're getting so much response. It was amazing to see what God was doing. We ministered all that we could.

Every time we give an invitation, hundreds would come forward. Hundreds of students who wanted to be our fire for Jesus and they were and they were winning souls right around them. UNC Greensboro, just everywhere.

God was moving. I remember being called in a youth conference meetings. I remember, one was like Joshua generation and was called to Kingston where I saw multiple revivals break out and high schools, junior highs and everywhere else.

I got invited to camp meetings in South Carolina where we're ministering to hundreds, if not thousands of students through Methodist camp meetings. They were just there for camp meeting and we were bringing them in for worship sets and for revival meetings. It was amazing what broke out from this.

Revival broke out and we did not stop until everyone else did. Do you have anything on that?

The only way to go from here is to be humble, and have integrity, and faithful, and be diligent.

We bring into this era, a wisdom saying, we know what went wrong last time, and we know how much not to touch the glory and instead to keep pleasing GOD. We are not great at this, but we are available and that is all GOD desires for you as well. Now, it is your turn. We have shared our story. We want to read yours that comes now!

All we know is that God's left us around so that we can help to shepherd and pastor the next generation. We're not here to do it again. We're here to see the next generation does it, we want to give our inheritance away, and we're here to make sure that they have the covering that we did not have.

Daniel: That's right.

Dustin: They'll have us, and we're here, and we're available, and we will keep our faces to the ground to make sure that they see God moving their era.

Daniel: Amen. I feel exactly the same way. I feel like it will be very meaningful to add a context.

Forwarded message:
From: ~~daniel@email.unc.edu~~ (Daniel Tan)
Sender: ~~daniel@email.unc.edu~~ (Daniel Tan)
To: FFire97@aol.com, ~~ghoonkim@email.unc.edu~~ (Chi-hyn Kim), ~~dkt7@aol.com~~,
DSHedrick@aol.com
Date: 97-02-21 04:50:05 EST

THIS IS AN EDITED VERSION THAT I WOULD RECOMMEND YOU KEEP AND FORWARD AS
YOU HAVE NEED. If you have editorial comments, please insert them and
mail this back to me.

Dan
-----Forward begins here-----

Please send this to anyone you think might be interested...

Many people have been asking, so here ya go...
This is as comprehensive as an unofficial update gets...
[An official update will be issued in late March, but until then, we'll
send word of news as we receive it]

THE FOREST FIRE 1997 UNOFFICIAL UPDATE...

An all-North Carolina, multi-campus praise night, Forest Fire 97, was just
held here at UNC-CH, hosted by In Christ Alone, an independent student
ministry here at UNC-CH (we started as an Asian ministry, but God has been
changing our focus to serve as bridge builders/ networkers for the past
year-and-a-half...).

It began with an opening song, and introduction, and two special guest
speakers: Robert Brickey, a former Duke basketball star, now working with
an inner city ministry in Fayetteville; and UNC-CH's own women's
basketball team coach, the legendary Sylvia Hatchell. During this time
and well into the first praise session, people continued to trickle-in,
bringing estimated attendance to 2500-3000 before the night was over.

Following that came a high-energy praise session led by the In Christ
Alone praise band.

Then, came CLAYTON KING, the main speaker. An energetic man, only
twenty-four, Clayton couldn't be contained by the stage and walked the
floor up close to the stands, literally talking face to face to those in
the audience. He spoke powerfully from the Word, reached into the Bible
and made it burst forth as the timeless words of Jesus came alive to all
present. He spoke on Matthew 6:25-34. "Therefore, I tell you, DO NOT

Page 1

93

WORRY..." He asked "why" we worried. "What" we were worried about. "Why" we couldn't trust Jesus when He told us plainly, "not to worry!" Clayton brought us into his life and showed us in a vivid way how God was working through him, and how meaningless our worries and fears were when God was so far greater than all of them... He spoke on life, on relationships, on choices, on joys, on humorous incidents, on serious ones, on tragedies... on a little of everything, and on a whole lot of Jesus Christ.

Then, he gave an invitation-- for those with burdens that they needed to lay before the Lord, and for those who wanted to accept Christ. Clayton said, "... no music, no playing off of your emotions, because yo' emotions cain't be trusted... " [paraphrase]

And then, he gave the most unusual invitation I have ever heard... "When I count to three, I want you to come forward..."

I couldn't believe my ears when he said that... And I held my breath, praying that God would move hearts, wondering all the while about this unconventional invitation.

He spoke for a little bit more, and then he started to count.

"One.." silence... He paused before he continued with,

"Two..." more silence. I couldn't hear any movement at all. Again, another pause. And then,

"Three."

And like a sudden gust of wind on a calm day, around 250 people rose as one and came down the aisles. I opened my eyes for just a moment, and I saw a sea of people kneeling in front of the stage. I have to confess... I closed my eyes, and I cried. I know that God worked in people's hearts. It wasn't emotionalism-- it was the conviction of the Holy Spirit... and it was powerful.

Of those on the floor, 50-60 were counselors-- some of whom came forward to make their hearts right before the Lord before they counseled others. A majority of people counseling were first-time counselors. I had several speak to me the week before Forest Fire, and they had said, "We're scared, but we're excited!" May God pour out blessings on those brave souls who said, "Here I am, Lord! I'm scared, but send me!"

Of people who came forward, some went back to their seats immediately, having made their peace with God right there in their hearts on the floor of Carmichael Auditorium. Some came to accept Christ. A large number of people coming forward came for rededication, to renew their commitment to Christ through confession. Some came for prayer, or had other needs. Some came to respond to God's calling to the ministry. Some came to know more about Jesus Christ. And there were many who stayed in the stands, who accepted Christ into their hearts when Clayton led them in prayer, and those who made their decisions in their hearts wherever they sat that night.

Respondees include junior highers (14 years old) as well as college and graduate school, full-time employed individuals, and locales as far

Page 2

94

ranging as Elon College, Duke, NC State, UNC-Chapel Hill, East Carolina University, Appalachian State, Wake Forest University, Campbell U, Stony Point, Statesville, Fayetteville, Boone, Virginia, Alabama, and Oklahoma City. There were a couple of other places, but I can't remember all of them.

That night, some counselors counseled one person, while some counselors counseled as many as four or five!

Counselors were all volunteers. God is AWESOME, God is GOOD! In Christ Alone is a small ministry with only 16 dedicated servants, but God brought so many volunteers--- ushers, setup/takedown crew, counselors, publicity contacts, etc...-- that we can't even begin to name them all! All-in-all, we must have had somewhere around 100 volunteers there, representing over ten different fellowship groups and ministries.

After the ICA Praise Band led a post-message praise session, two Christian bands in this area gave a free concert-- Mark Williams, and Big Wednesday.

Overall, it was, well, kind of overwhelming for us all. But God tends to do that... Yup. God can be quite overwhelming sometimes...

"For we walk by faith, not by sight." (II Cor. 5:7) Forest Fire 97 started by faith in the Lord's provision and power. It began at Wake Forest University in March of last year with the conviction that the Lord wanted to touch hearts for His kingdom's sake through it. This year, He forced the 1997 host ministry, In Christ Alone, to our knees before Him, again and again until we had totally surrendered the night to Him. Forest Fire 97 was not about ICA, Clayton King, Mark Williams, Big Wednesday, Robert Brickey, Sylvia Hatchell. Forest Fire 97 was about God speaking to the hearts of individuals through His Words. Nothing else mattered, nothing else matters, and nothing else will matter except for the decisions made, the lives that were changed, and the eternal purposes for that night. Only God knows what He plans to do with the spark that He ignited that Saturday evening.

A big prayer request is for those who made decisions-- that the decisions made will be LIFE-CHANGING. Pray for counselors as they follow-up on those who came forward. Pray for CONSISTENCY in the lives of counselors AND those who made decisions. And PRAISE GOD for His faithfulness!! He is UNBELIEVABLE!

One small prayer request is that we still need to raise funds to cover all the expenses for the event. In short, the event was not cheap, but God has already told us He will provide, so we're trusting by faith that He will. A gazillion fund-raising letters have already gone out the door, and a whole lot of people know about the need already...

SOME ANECDOTES THAT I'VE HEARD...

I've been hearing many things that have really encouraged me through these past few days...

Someone who was in the lobby area said that half-an-hour into the praise session, a young lady left the auditorium in tears, accompanied by two of her friends who supported her. A friend of mine who brought three non-Christian friends said that one of her friends was moved to tears by

Page 3

95

the praise, saying, ""I've never heard anything like it before!" This
same friend of mine also said that one of her friends later confessed that
she had wanted to go forward on Saturday to accept Christ, but she didn't.
Well, she accepted Christ two days later instead !

I also heard (the video records should confirm it) that when Clayton
asked people to raise their hands for acceptance, that fifty hands went up
(this was a confession from someone who said they 'peeked' when everyone
else's eyes were closed!). Pray for those who did not speak to a
counselor, but who remained in the stands, that they may be surrounded by
strong Christian fellowship as they start their new walk wherever they
are.

I heard a couple of people say, "I saw people who I thought would NEVER
come to a Christian meeting in attendance that night!" I know I had some
friends who haven't been in a church in years who came that night.

A young man who has watched his own flesh-and-blood brother struggle with
drug addiction and alcohol over the past few years saw God break through
to his brother's heart that night. God broke the hold of drugs and
alcohol on his life and this brother came forward and dedicated his life
to Christ.

If you are in Charlotte, and you listen to country, please confirm this...
Clayton mentioned that someone called him and told him that a man called
up the largest country music station in Charlotte during one of the live
call-in segments, and started going off on how his life had been changed
at Forest Fire 97 just that past weekend.

By the way, little trivia note, the farthest locations represented were
probably Alabama, Texas, Oklahoma City, and California. At least one
person from Oklahoma City flew out specifically for Forest Fire. The
Californians were visiting in the area and came on out with a local
pastor.

A lot of people have been saying that Forest Fire really encouraged and
refreshed them, and one person said, "Did you notice how diverse the crowd
was? And when people talked to each other, it was like it really didn't
matter who you were or where you were from. That was sooo incredible!"

Anyways, those are just a few anecdotes that I've been hearing lately...
Let me know what you hear as well! Please email us at FFire97@aol.com to
let us know your thoughts, testimonies, comments... If you know of
someone who came forward who needs some solid follow-up material, have
them contact us, and we would be glad to send some material their way.

If you received follow-up material, the "Living in Christ" book, please
complete the lessons-- we GUARANTEE it will help provide a strong,
Biblical foundation for future commitments and growth-- and fill in and
send-in the postcard in the back of the flap to receive a free gift from
the Billy Graham Association (well worth it, I assure you!).

May God richly bless you as you seek to know Him more! Keep in touch,
brothers and sisters. Support the body of Christ, wherever you are at,
because God has great things in store if His people will only seek after
His kingdom...

Page 4

Well, I better go... Take care, keep in touch, PRAISE GOD, THANK YOU LORD GOD, JESUS CHRIST, AND THE HOLY SPIRIT!

I think everyone in ICA needs a long sabbatical right about now...

In Christ Alone,
                Dan Tan
on behalf of the Forest Fire 97 planning crew
Dustin Hedrick, G-hoon Kim, and Jeff Lin
and on behalf of In Christ Alone Ministries.
Please feel free to email us at FFire97@aol.com!

~~~~~~

In Christ Alone is an independent student ministry at UNC-CH whose goals are to promote interaction between Bible-believing Christian groups for the sake of the gospel of Jesus Christ, across racial, denominational, and geographic lines.

Forest Fire exists independently of In Christ Alone, and is sponsored by a different campus and ministry each year. Forest Fire 97 is the second annual Forest Fire event. For more information, slightly outdated though, please see our website at http://users.aol.com/FFire97

Forest Fire is not affiliated with any of the Billy Graham Associate Crusades. The Billy Graham Training Center in Asheville, NC, provided counselor training for this event, but the BGEA (Billy Graham Evangelistic Association) is not responsible for Forest Fire 97. Counselor training consisted of the "Christian Life and Witness Course," and is the same training provided for Billy Graham Associate Crusades counselors around the world. By the way, for a solid Christian LIFE, GROWTH, and WITNESS course, ICA would HIGHLY recommend the CL&W Course, which is a four-part course. No previous experience is necessary.
~~~~~~

Page 5

TO: RRISS RRISS@drew.edu

Subject: Forest Fire 97

Mr. Riss,

My name is Dustin Hedrick. I am 22 years old and I love Jesus more than anything in the world. I am a youth evangelist from Stony Point, North Carolina. I am out of the Southern Baptist Church.

Two years ago I attended the Toronto Airport Vineyard and this past year I attended Brownsville Assemblies of God. I was skeptical at first, but God really changed my life when He touched me at Toronto. Now, I am going to a diverse group of people back to Brownsville from some of the NC college campuses!

Since then I have been on fire for the Lord and have sought ways to see Him glorified. This brings me to why I am writing. I am now the coordinator for Forest Fire 97. Which is a multi-ethnic, multi-campus, and multi-denominational conference in which all the 32? campus Christian groups

Page 1

at UNC-Chapel Hill got together to praise the Lord along with people from all over the US and world that are attending high school or college.

It all started when we had Christ Awareness Week on campus, (Feb. 10th-14th). We had the different campus Christian organizations pull together to show that we are unified in Christ. And that we love Jesus more than anything and that He loves them.

All week we had speakers and singing in the central meeting place on the campus. Over 20,000 people attend UNC, so who knows how many people heard the gospel of Jesus Christ! On the last day, students from other college campuses even came in to give their testimonies, telling for the first time about their lives sharing about things such as how they had been raped or into various sins, such as premarital sex, and drugs. Some even gave testimonies on how they had been healed of different spiritual and physical things. One girl even got up and told for the first time to anyone how she had been raped and how through Jesus touching her life just recently, she had forgiven the person who did it!

And this is only the beginning!

On February 15, 1997, over 3000 people came into Carmichael auditorium for Forest Fire 97. It took place on the UNC-Chapel Hill campus. The reason we had this event was to promote unity and to see revival. WE WANT REVIVAL IN OUR SCHOOLS!

The people who attended were from schools like: Liberty University, UNC-Chapel Hill, UNC-Charlotte, ECU, Wake Forest University, Elon College, Duke University, NC State University, Meredith College, UNC- Greensboro, Appalachian State University, University of Georgia, Campbell University and Universities in Alabama, Oklahoma, Illinois, Indiana, Maryland, Virginia. There were people from youth groups from all over North Carolina also.

Coach Sylvia Hatchell, the women's basketball coach (whose team is ranked 5th in the nation), and Robert Brickey the Young Life coordinator from Durham, who played for the Duke Blue Devils Basketball team were our opening speakers. Our main speaker was Clayton King, (the most phenomenal youth evangelist I have ever heard).

When Clayton King gave the invitation, without any music or words spoken, over 250 people came forward to rededicate their lives to the Lord and to be saved!!! PRAISE GOD! (Pardon my excitement). Not only that, but throughout the service, the Lord was moving. I can honestly say that people were being touched by the Lord.

A bunch of the students who attended from ECU and Appalachian came back with me to my house and we had some real prayer time. In this time, they got really excited to go back to their schools and see them won for Jesus. We are already planning ways that we can go into other schools and share our testimonies and tell people about Jesus and see that they get touched by the Lord so that they can take their schools..

Now, there is an excitement that is spreading all over campuses everywhere about what people can do to serve the Lord and know Him more! There is a growing unity like never before at UNC and am excited to see Jesus being lifted up at other campuses.

Page 2

God is doing awesome things and we are going to keep working to see that He keeps doing it. There is still much to do, so pray for more.

We want God to take back the public schools. I want to give my life to see that He does. Our Youth need Jesus and they need Him in a powerful way just like what we are seeing at Toronto and Pensacola. That is what they want!.

Praise the Lord,
In His Grip,
Dustin Hedrick
DSHedrick@aol.com

18 REKINDLED
JANUARY 2013

At the time of this recording, we are currently driving back up from UNC Chapel Hill back to Washington, DC where our base is. The reason this is important is not because this was some sort of a planned strategic move.

This was something that was stirring in our hearts. Today, the day was Sunday, January 20th, 2013. After a great worship service in the morning...

Dustin: God's presence fell.

Daniel: ...God's presence fell...

Dustin: ...teaching on the Kingdom, too.

Daniel: That's right. When we were done, with all the ministry work, and we came outside, we decided we have to drop everything and go to UNC, because we are supposed to check in with GOD, at this point.

Dustin: Check in for duty.

Daniel: It's exactly what we did. That's why we drove down to Carolina. The LORD had miraculously already given us a contact down there. That's another story...

Dustin: That's another story, for another show.

Daniel: Perhaps you could bring it in.

Dustin: Yeah, maybe I'll do it in a minute.

19 THE FIRE'S EFFECT
SPRING 1997

Dustin: Amen. I'll say this, giving a context that even what happened in Carolina campus, like we said in the beginning in 1993, we only had a couple hundred meeting at these campus ministries. And when we were done in 1997, InterVarsity was so large, it did not fit in the whole great hall. It was over 1,200 for the last meetings it had.

Campus crusade had grown so large, and listen, this was not directly related to Forest Fire. It was directly related to a stirring across the campus through prayer, fasting, worship, which we had Pit praises, I forgot to mention. Leading into forest fire, we had multiple times where G-hoon and Dan Tan would step out, do worship in the middle of this central meeting place, the campus and pit.

Over and over, they did this and hundreds worshiped together just in the open air. Not planned. Just drop everything and have Pit praise. Sometimes they would even send out a flyer, saying, "pit praise... @ this time," and people just come out, and just seeing whatever was done and there'd be pit praise.

Those stirrings, the prayer meetings, the pit praise, Forest Fire, literally overtly or covertly, affected campus ministries at UNC and they exploded by Spring 1997. They grew Crusade for Christ so that it couldn't meet at Gerard. They had to meet at the amphitheater.

Everything exploded, everything was big. And we preached in the Pit for the rest of the time when I was there.

When I go out to that pit preach anytime GOD told me, it would be hundreds of people out and listen and they weren't yelling and screaming, and cursing. They didn't know me, but at the same time they would listen.

Christians got where we would help each other, so Christians would hear me preach or hear even Gary Birdsong who was, oh my gosh, horrible, and does not have the love of God in him at all. He may not be even a Christian. He's hardening hearts, but by preaching the Bible.

We would get off to the side and use him and preach to those around us and literally leap it with Jesus, but there were thousands affected. It went from hundreds to thousands affected in Carolina.

We were invited all over after that. The emails came in with all the outflow of what had happened and we were immediately thrown into full blown ministry with full blown schedules from the coast of NC to the mountains. We found ourselves driving from one end of the state to the other, speaking at campus after campus, sharing the story of what GOD had done at Carolina and ministering to spread the fire.

A few I remember are, UNC Charlotte, East Carolina University, Appalachian State University, UNC Greensboro, other colleges and Universities from even other states like Iowa State University. We had so many invites to youth events, campuses, youth groups, college groups and churches. I would often speak in a church and go into the schools and speak to students on making good decisions and we would have revival spread into the schools. One school, the principal sent all the worst kids in first. They had run off the last speaker they had by not listening and booing, etc. These 500 students ended up responding to a call I had at the end for counseling. THE WHOLE ROOM came forward!!!! The principal called me in, introduced me to the superintendent of schools, told me to preach the whole Gospel, sent every kid through the rest of the day to various other assemblies and then asked me to stay in the hall and minister to the kids through the end of the day. The church that I spoke at during the evenings was bombarded by day's end for our information because other teachers heard and begged me to speak at their schools and churches and the church went into revival where every meeting did not have room for everyone that came.

We would speak and minister at a University such as Wake Forest and I remember G-hoon had to extract me from the meeting during the ministry time because we had to leave to be able to make it across state to go to class the next day and to go to another place to speak the next day. He used to say, "You preach and I will drive…" He still drives!

These meetings grew and grew and we saw more and more. We had not even graduated and we were thrown into full-blown revival meetings. We began to expect GOD's Presence to be at an event we went to and to take over. We expected massive amounts of salvations and massive altar calls. We expected responses.

One meeting in Charlotte, NC we did where G-hoon led worship and I spoke, GOD's Presence came so strong during the second night that there was a gang who had come to attend to make fun of what was happening and they sat at the back. They literally disappeared during the invitation at the end of the meeting. During that invitation, every person in the audience came forward for salvation or rededication to the LORD. I looked at the back and someone was coming forward and that was some feat since there was no room for them to walk up since the aisles were full of people and there was no room to step. This person came up, told us there was a gang here that needed ministry. We could not see them. I (Dustin) went back to the back and I asked where they were. The person said they are under the back pew. They were afraid to come forward. They felt that GOD was so real that HE might kill them if they did. They were saved right there. They all repented and asked JESUS into their hearts. GOD had come and HE was on us wherever we went.

We used to have a heavy Presence wherever we were in ministry so that people even sometimes would come up and just ask for us to lead them to JESUS not even knowing who we were. It was crazy! And I would preach anywhere. I even preached in restaurants after a few of us were excited sharing what JESUS was doing. I went in the back one time I remember and spoke to the entire staff and they all responded and were affected rather than kicking me out. Once, the waitress accepted JESUS in the middle of taking an order when I said that her smile must mean she was happy… She broke down and said she wasn't and accepted JESUS on the spot.

GOD had come and we had to keep going and keep sharing anywhere we were invited and that ended up being NC, SC, GA primarily and then all over. This of course led to my being ordained into full time ministry right after graduation from college even though I had not even had seminary. The denomination thought it best since like it or not, we were ministering on a large basis.

GOD WAS NEAR! HE IS COMING NEAR AGAIN!!!!!!

It just needs to be understood, out of 30,000 undergrads and with graduate students, 40,000 students in Carolina, there were thousands and thousands affected by the Kingdom of God in a very short period of time. In less than one year's time, that happened.

Subj: FFire97
Date: Thu, Feb 20, 1997 2:07 PM EDT
From: ▓▓▓▓▓▓▓▓▓▓▓▓▓▓▓

X-From: ▓▓▓▓▓▓▓▓▓▓▓▓ (Daniel Tan)
Sender: ▓▓▓▓▓▓▓▓▓▓▓▓▓▓▓▓
Reply-to: ▓▓▓▓▓▓▓▓▓▓▓▓▓▓▓▓
To: ▓▓▓▓▓▓▓▓▓▓▓▓▓▓

I've been hearing from Clayton that he's already getting letters and phone calls from people whose lives were changed at Forest Fire. Someone contacted him and told him that some guy in Charlotte called the largest country music station there and , while on the air, went off about how his life was radically changed by Forest Fire this past weekend.

I sent out that "little" update about Forest Fire yesterday, that contains some of the things I've been hearing. We'll be in touch with Clayton soon, though, and we'll see how things were from his perspective... PRAY FOR FOLLOW-UP!

Dan

Subject: Forest Fire update

Mr. Riss,

I just wanted to keep you updated on what is going on and lift Jesus up.

We have been getting many emails from people from all over that are telling
about how God is moving on their campuses in mighty ways.

We are also hearing from people all over North Carolina that are testifying
to what the Lord has done in their lives. One person whos did this is from
Charlotte, NC. This person was touched at Forest Fire, so when he got home
Monday morning, he called in to one of the area's largest Country radio
stations and told "on the air" how God had changed his life at Forest Fire!
Someone else in Charlotte heard the broadcast and called the speaker,
(Clayton King) about it! So, who knows how many lost people heard that
testimony!

Clayton says that he has received numerous messages and letters saying
that
God changed people's lives at Forest Fire. He is presently travelling all
over the area and the US and world spreading the gospel. It seems that
wherever he goes, God is faithful to move. If anyone would like additional
information about how to contact Clayton, his number is ████████████

This past Thurday, at The University of North Carolina at Chapel Hill. over
1240 people came together to be at a racial reconciliation conference in
which all of the campus groups again participated. The speakers for this
event were the authors of the book "More Than Equals." At this conference,
people really were able to come together in unity despite our different
races. God is really doing some great things here.

This past weekend, I was invited to go to Greenville, NC to be at a meeting
at East Carolina University. This state university has approximately

3/4/97   America Online: DSHedrick   Page 2

106

18,000
students.

At this meeting on Saturday morning at 10:00AM, people from the various
campus groups came together to take a prayer walk across their campus.
It
took approximately 3 and a half hours and it was awesome. The people
were a
bold witness to other students on the campus and they prayed and sang
praises
across the campus. We prayed for every building on the campus and
consecrated
them to the Lord, so that He might use them for His glory. They want to
see
the power of God made manifest at their school in whatever way the Lord
wants
to do it.

Some of the groups i think were represented were IVCF, Campus Christian
Fellowship, and the Baptist Student Union and I am not sure which other
ones
were represented.

That evening we had a Bible study that lasted about 5 hours! I ministered
on
how we must have a intimate relationship with the Holy Spirit of God. The
Lord was gracious to come and heal some hurts in people's lives. The Lord
has
so much more in store for this school!

They are also planning a gathering for all of the campus groups called
EARTHQUAKE. We will be conducting an outdoor service, so the lost can
hear
the Word. They say that they want their campus to be shaken for Jesus
Christ.
They are really praying for revival.

The main leader's name is Randy Greene and his email is
~~GROREENE@ecuvm.cis.ecu.edu~~ In case anyone would like additional
information
on the event.

This weekend my co-coordinator, (G-Hoon Kim) and I will be going to UNC
at
Charlotte and we will be leading some services down there. Soon we will
be
going to Appalachian State University and some other universities. It
seems
that people are praying all over for revival. And God is doing mighty things
accross this state.

This next week, instead of going out and wasting our time partying over
spring break, we are taking a group from ECU and from UNC Chapel Hill to
Pensacola. We want to bring the fire back with us, so we can take our
campuses for Jesus.

Though professors, this world and our peers may pour water over our
wood, our
God is the God who burns wet wood! (See 1Kings 18:30-39).

I pray that God continues to spread the fire to our college campuses. As
for
now, I pray for more!

Thanks so much for all of the encouragement,

God bless,
Dustin Hedrick
DSHedrick@aol.com

20 THE NEXT GENERATION NOW

Daniel: (About Charlotte, a student at Chapel Hill). We went down there, we were bringing new contacts to her, we were helping her understand what needs to be done. It wasn't about, "This is what you need to do, one, two, three," but I think we were coaching her to just look at God and focus on the Lord and stop focusing on other things.

We were praying over her, we were praying together, we were giving her the coverage, and then, at the moment, we were driving back out. We are just driving through the night right now. This is very significant because this moment right here, as we record, this will be remembered as the beginning of the second phase.

Now, one more piece for the context to the story. We started praying into what God was calling us to do with this story, and with the next year, and we felt like it wasn't over.

We had to pray in to how we could pass this onto into the next generation. We didn't know what to do. We just knew that we had to give this away and we had to pass some of the inheritance. It's not about us. We want it to happen again, and again, and again, and again.

Just like that 1970's recording by Dennis Kinlaw, this recording will be something that speaks into the next generation and our voices will be as well. So we start talking about it. What do we do? G-hoon says to me, "Just pray. We'll pray and you'll know when God brings the right person to you."

I was thinking, "In the church or whatever?" He said, "Just pray. God will bring her or God will bring him and it'll be the person, just the contact for UNC. They'll come in your church." He's just like, "God will bring them. We'll pray God brings them." I'm like, "OK."

I'm not thinking anything about it. About a week later, I'm talking to the leadership about getting a flag sign for outside. I thought it would be cool. It was different and it was easy to put up and down.

They thought it'd be a waste. I told it wasn't a waste. Even if no one came, that we needed to have our presence out there, but I said to them, "We don't know. God may bring one person. The one person we need to reach and one person is worth the flag." They said, "OK, fine."

I pushed through it and I got it anyway. I put the flag out the first week. The first week the flag's out, a young lady by the name of Charlotte Jackson, saw it at the road and thought to herself, "I want to go check this place out next," during her break.

She comes back the next week and comes into our church. She's starting to talk to people and they're introducing themselves and she explains it. She's just there for the weekend because she's got to go back to Carolina to go to school.

I had thought up to this point that when G-hoon said that someone would come, that he is crazy. I thought, "How in the world would someone going to UNC come to Washington, DC to my church and how I'm I going to know it's them? This is ridiculous."

This girl walks in and my people at the church, my family there or the church members say, "You need to meet our pastor. You've got to meet him immediately. He loves Carolina. Has a heart for it."

She comes up to me and she says, "I think I'm supposed to meet you. They said I should let you know I go to Carolina." I said, "You go to Carolina. Are you kidding me?"

She said, "No." I responded, "Oh my goodness. This is crazy. God sent you." She replies, "Really." I said, "What do you do at Carolina?" She says, "Well, I'm going to be one of the leaders for InterVarsity Christian Fellowship and I'm currently on the worship team."

I was blown away. I said, "Oh my goodness. You got to be kidding me." She's says, "Why?" I said, "Because we're called to pass on this inheritance to those who will come after us. It's from this thing called Forest Fire '97 which was a revival that broke out in Carolina and it came through Wake Forest University, thus Forest Fire, and it came through InterVarsity Christian Fellowship."

I said, "That's your inheritance and my friend just prophesied to me a week and a half ago, two weeks ago, that you would come and here you are." She responds, "You got to be kidding." I said, "No."

Tonight when we dropped everything, we drove down G-hoon was saying, "I did not have her information. I had one email in my inbox that I was able to search and find on my iPhone.

I pull that out, search for her on Facebook as we're driving down there because we weren't ready to meet. I had nothing. I pulled out Facebook and

I found her on Facebook, like a hundred Charlotte Jacksons. I went through and I felt, "Oh my God, please Lord, help me find her. How do I know it's her?"

I found one Charlotte Jackson that had two friends in common. I thought, "Wow. People from Tapestry. She must have made friends." It wasn't Tapestry, but it was Charlotte Jackson.

When I clicked through, it was two other people. One was from Ichthus Church, a different church that she doesn't know about me that she went to school with at her high school in Maryland and the other is Troutman Baptist church in North Carolina that she's come across that she's been in Carolina.

Both people are in my Facebook. They were the two in common and they were the ones that brought her up the top of the list so I could pick her out and we could find her.

I found her, I added her. She had her phone on her. She said she just pulled it out randomly, added me as her friend, message me, I message back. We met with her, prayed for and bam, come on Jesus, revival and we're in it, and so Forest Fire, game on. Game on...

So, it begins again...

AFTERWARDS
WHAT DO WE DO NOW?

Have your own forest fire! The reason we have no revival in our time is because we can still live without it.

AN EXPERIMENT:
This is not a new idea and we will not take credit for it. It is based on the Asbury 1970 Revival story. However, this is the experiment. We encourage everyone to do the following and let's see what happens.

HERE IS ONE MORE LINK TO THE ASBURY REVIVAL VIDEO BY DENNIS KENLAW THAT AFFECTED US SO MUCH

1 – Find one or two other people that you will covenant with to pray together.

2 – Agree to pray personally for 10-30 minutes per day for GOD to bring his Manifest Presence on your campus, bringing awareness to people as well as a Spirit of salvation and growth to all Christian groups and unity between all Christians and Christian groups on the campus.

3 – Look for opportunities to join GOD where HE is working as well as opportunities to share your faith daily. This includes simply doing kindness acts and sharing Jesus, or like we did, it may be preaching in open air, doing some kind of servanthood to share about Jesus or an awareness week, or open air spontaneous worship. It could as well include something someone else is doing that GOD shows you that you can join them in. If someone else is doing worship, you can jump in and sing with them. If someone is preaching, you can get in the crowd and pull people to the side to share the Gospel when they seem to be seeking or GOD is working on their hearts. I used to do this and people accepted Jesus even when really bad preachers were preaching and making people mad. GOD can change anything for HIS good. Just, watch and join HIM.

4 – Meditate on Scripture every day as well as reading the Bible. You can use devotionals such as "The Experiencing GOD Devotional" by Henry Blackaby, "Morning & Evening" by Charles Spurgeon or "My Utmost to HIS Highest," by Oswald Chambers.

5 – Get together every week for 30 minutes with your partners in ministry and don't get together to just talk about your week, but sincerely pray for revival together for GOD to move on your campus. Name names and ask for details. Dream big. Pray big. And take time for GOD to speak to each of you and share it as you are done. The focus is on GOD and not on you getting your needs met. So, you are sacrificially praying for GOD to move and asking GOD what HE wants.

6 – Take time to fast alone and together. You can fast and pray and come into alignment with HIS will. If you need more information on fasting, IHOP in Kansas City has wonderful resources, or you can get my book, "The Warrior's Manual."

7 – Begin to ask GOD what HE will do on your campus. Prepare to make a plan for something big and begin to ask GOD to open your eyes. You may be called to a big thing like a Forest Fire event or something else GOD tells you. Whatever it is, let us know if we can help!

8 – Live different. As GOD draws you to love HIM more and as HE reveals where you are lacking, you agree to change into more of HIS desire and image.

9 – Worship. Bow down who you are and do it alone as well as in unity with others. DO NOT only worship in public. Jesus always said to do your stuff in private more than public. So, there you go.

So, that is the beginning. This is a covenant plan. I promise you that even if it takes 4 years as it did with us, it is worth it. Just watch what GOD can do. And now, here is a little more of the values and priorities of the movement. That is the experiment. This is the character behind it.

THE FOREST FIRE REKINDLED 3 STEP PLAN:
"Rekindled"

We are asking you to come with us on this journey of rekindling a generation in your generation to seek GOD's face. We understand that this is a book written in a certain time and time will go on and people will question the framing of this book as well as its relevance for the time they live in. The truth is that GOD's Truth is not an idea or a simple concept. It is not framed by a time or a culture. Truth is a person. HIS name is Jesus! And the works of the Kingdom as well as the characteristics and the priorities below are not reliant on a certain era or culture. They are transcultural and timeless. With that said, here they are.

CHARACTERISTICS OF REKINDLING A KINGDOM MOVEMENT

Presence - We are seeking the Jesus Life, which is relationship with Holy Spirit, leading to fruitful lives. (You can find the basis in Scripture in Matthew 5-7 and John 13-17). The fruit comes out of outflow of relationship and is the fruit of the Spirit. Over time, this discipled or disciplined life leads to maturity of faith. These obedient servants will carry the Manifest Presence of GOD. We are after a manifested, real Presence of GOD in our lives or they encounter GOD physically and spiritually when they are around us.

Prayer - 2x2 - As Jesus said, where two or more gather in my name, I am in the midst of them. We seek GOD together for revival on our campuses specifically, purposefully, faithfully and diligently with expectancy and desperation.

Practice - M68 - The Practices of Justice are not possible without proximity to the Presence of GOD. There is an attitude like Moses that we will not leave this mountain unless HE goes before us. And as Jesus sent out the disciples 2x2, we go preaching the Gospel, and demonstrating the Kingdom.

To do justice, we must first be justified as well as just. I am calling people in this era not so simply go out and do justice but to walk near GOD, hear HIS desire, join HIM in HIS justice work and to start with being just in our hearts through fighting lusts and addictions and fighting against any compulsion to treat another human as an object versus a person or to dehumanize them through pornography or whatever we do to fill our needs, consuming their person in order to feed our desires, compulsions and more. In other words, if you want to fight injustices in sex trafficking, start with not consuming porn. We undercut the whole thing if we do not consume it. If something is not in demand, then it will not be supplied.

And we can start to fight this even before porn. What about a movement to fight against using another person to get our needs met even in our daily lives. Fighting manipulation. Fighting for chastity. Fighting for people to wait for marriage. Fighting for our sisters and brothers not to be used and abused and thrown to the side like a dirty diaper.

Make this covenant with me which encapsulates the whole of our movement:
"We will Do Justly, Love Mercy, Walk Humbly before our GOD."

READ THESE AUTHORS & BOOKS FOR MORE:
Leonard Ravenhill
Henry Blackaby
Oswald Chambers
Charles Finney
"Firefall" by Alvin Reid
Find the video about Asbury 1970 with Dennis Kenlaw
J. Edwin Orr

ALSO GO TO OUR WEBSITE TO JOIN THE MOVEMENT:
www.TheForestFire.org

APPENDIX
THE FOREST FIRE ARCHIVES

We just had to add these stories and snippets from what had built up to the event. This is a part of our record for the generations after us.

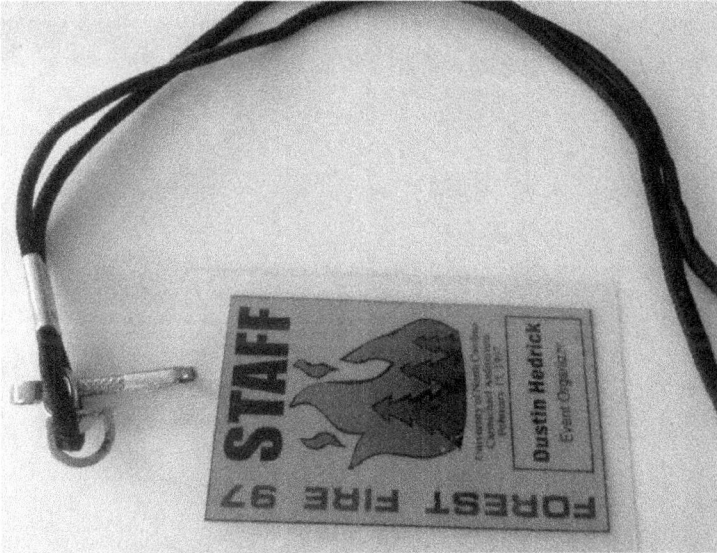

All of our prayer team, In Christ Alone Praise team and staff had to have these badges to get around back stage as well as before while we setup for the event. (We thought these were cutting edge for our time).

The Temple Times

February 1997

A Message From Dustin

Forest Fire 97

Power To Fuel Evangelism

Happy Birthday!

R. L. Mitchell - 4
Carl Buttle - 5
Charles Miller - 9
Tansy Levan - 10
Maxine Stone - 11
Doris Fox - 12
Jamie Gilreath - 16
Tonya Mayberry - 16
Carolyn Marlowe - 18
Tanya Baker - 21
Rosie Adams - 22
Marilyn Weeks - 25
Roger Lackey - 26
Lelia Panks - 26
Donn Rogers - 27
Lou Ann Mitchell - 28
Ted Weeks - 28

Temple Baptist Church's monthly newsletter with the pastor's notes about the event as well as my letter to the church:

See:
"A Message from Dustin"

"Forest   Fire   97"

118

These were some of the posters we plastered the campus with.

The team began to place flyers like these as well as many other designs on bright colored paper all over the campus starting in November through December on random nights weekly and then daily before the event in February. We would go to bed and wake to 1000's of these posters for FF97 everywhere.

They were on trees, poles, signs, the bricks on the walkway, laid out in designs and grids everywhere. The campus all over looked like whatever color the posters were. No one could miss them. One of my favorites said, "The   Fire   is   Coming!"

This is the official event poster all in color, which was very expensive back then. Fun Facts:

The background was the song, "Light the Fire Again."

The email was AOL.

The website was pre-customized domains everywhere era.

The picture of Clayton King was actually a famous movie star since we did not have his picture yet.

And Jeff Linn did all the graphics.

Come in from the cold and join students with their...

...*Hearts Afire*...

FREE CONCERT

FOREST FIRE FOREST FORESTFIRE FOREST FIRE FIREFORESTFIRE FIRE FOREST FIRE

DANGER FLAMMABLE

Clayton King

ICA Praise Band

Robert Brickey

Big Wednesday

Mark Williams

CARMICHAEL AUDITORIUM @UNC
February 15, 1997
7 pm
http://users.aol.com/ffire97

This is another of the many different kinds of posters we plastered everywhere over campus. The sideways cross text was so cutting edge since graphic design was just then taking off on computers. We used every technology   GOD   gave   us   access   to.

The Herald-Sun

the chapel hill Herald

FEBRUARY 2, 1997   SUNDAY   VOL. 9, NO. 236

An edition of The Herald-Sun, Durham, N.C.

Christian students on a UNC mission

By SUSAN BROILI
The Chapel Hill Herald

CHAPEL HILL — Organizers hope up to 10,000 Christian college students will converge on UNC for the second annual Forest Fire Conference later this month.

UNC Women's Basketball Coach Sylvia Hatchell will open the Feb. 15 conference in Carmichael Auditorium at 7 p.m., which also features former Duke basketball player Robert Brickey and Baptist minister Clayton King.

HATCHELL

UNC senior Dustin Hedrick, conference coordinator, said the name has nothing to do with putting out forest fires, but rather with starting a fire — metaphorically speaking.

The conference originated last year at Wake Forest University in Winston-Salem and drew 600 students.

"They wanted the fire to start at Wake Forest — a fire as far as the Christian community pulling together and letting the world know. Not only in race and denomination, but in spirit, we're together as a body for the purpose of praising God," Hedrick said, his voice hoarse from preaching at a Charlotte youth revival over the weekend.

Hatchell said she readily agreed to appear at the conference.

please see CONFERENCE/7

This is the front page of the Chapel Hill Herald. This was the Sunday edition and was one of the many papers we ended up being featured and reported in. They covered the story on February 2, 1997. This raised the profile of the event immensely. Word spread fast and before it was over, we were on radio, print and even were interviewed on TV.

CONFERENCE FROM 1

"I support what they're doing. Anytime I can participate in anything that will enrich the lives of the students and direct them in a positive, Christian way, I'll do it," Hatchell said.

Hatchell said she thinks it helps being a Christian coach.

"You build a lot of character. You always have an inspiration type thing for yourself or the kids," Hatchell said.

The Tar Heel women pray before and after every game.

"And not necessarily to win," Hatchell said. "I pray that no one gets hurt, that I, as a coach, will have the knowledge to do a good job ... that we play hard, play smart and play together."

Hatchell, coach at UNC since 1986, said her players decided to pray after games, with players taking turns saying prayers of "thanksgiving – whether we win or lose, to keep us unified and healthy."

The next time they'll be praying and playing will be at 2 p.m. today when they meet Wake Forest in Winston-Salem.

The team is ranked sixth nationally, with a record of 18-1, and ranked first in the ACC, with a record of 9-0. Hatchell's 1993-4

team won the NCAA women's basketball championship, and she was named the National Coach of the Year by "USA Today" and "College Sports Magazine."

Both Hatchell and Hedrick spoke of the approximately 30 strong Christian groups on campus, including Athletes in Action and the Fellowship of Christian Athletes, and said they expect many members at the conference.

Hedrick attributed the high number of group participants to a growing Christian movement among young people.

"I think our generation is realizing that God is real and we are really seeing Jesus Christ as our Lord and Savior," Hedrick said.

The Statesville native, who said he grew up in the Southern Baptist Church and was called to preach about three years ago, said that young Christians are working to right wrongs in society.

"There's a lot of things in society that could use help – anything from murder, rape, incest. There's a lot of anger and violence. The Christian community finally sees that they are the hope for the nation, the Lord Jesus Christ is the hope for the nation," Hedrick said.

"I just hope I see more happiness

on campus and more people caring about each other and reaching out and helping each other," he added. "I'd just like to see more people my age reach out to the younger generation."

Hedrick said campus Christian groups are active in the community.

New Vision Church, a campus interdenominational church begun about a year ago, is working with at-risk children, while the Intervarsity Christian Fellowship is working on race relations, Hedrick said.

The conference, sponsored by family radio station WRTP AM 1530, is free, but a collection will be taken to defray the $20,000 cost, Hedrick said. Though the conference is targeting students, the general public may also attend.

The event will last until midnight and include concerts by Big Wednesday and Mark Williams. Eugene Lee and the In Christ Alone Praise Band will lead worship and Knights for Christ, a drama group based in Stony Point, will perform "Arise, My Love."

For more information about the conference, call Dustin Hedrick at 932-3045

(The second page of the Herald's story covering the event).

ORANGE COUNTY

Organizers hope to attract 10,000 to Christian gathering

By SUSAN BROILI
The Herald-Sun

SYLVIA HATCHELL:
"Anytime I can participate in anything that will enrich the lives of the students and direct them in a positive, Christian way, I'll do it."

This is the Herald-Sun's coverage for the larger Orange County area.

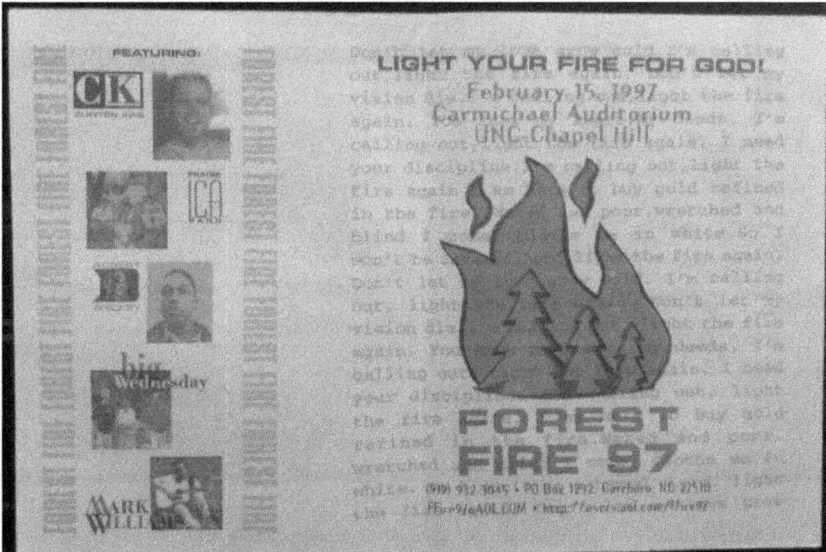

The full sized event poster was an 11x17 poster with three-color print. Again, this was cutting edge for college students and costly. Clayton's real picture finally makes it into this one.

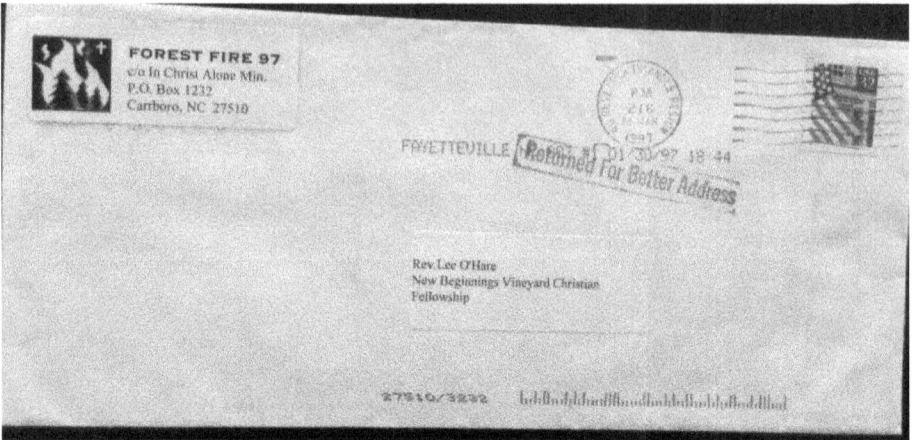

FOREST FIRE 97
c/o In Christ Alone Min.
P.O. Box 1232
Carrboro, NC 27510

FAYETTEVILLE Returned For Better Address

Rev. Lee O'Hare
New Beginnings Vineyard Christian
Fellowship

27310/3232

This is the letter we sent out to the pastors all over our area. We sent these letters mainly to the triangle area but also sent some to areas at the coast of NC as well as the mountains. We really did not know what to expect, we just wanted college students to hear about this thing.

COME CELEBRATE THE REASON FOR THE SEASON!

I bring you good news of great joy that will be for all the people. Today in the town of David a Savior has been born to you: He is Christ the Lord. Luke 2: 10-11

ALL-CAMPUS
PRAISE &
WORSHIP

In Christ Alone

GERRARD
HALL

ACROSS FROM
THE OLD WELL,
UNC-CH

For more information or
directions to UNC, e-mail:
ica@email.unc.edu

NOV. 23
6:30PM

This event was one of the all campus praise events in November before Christmas break.

We did events such as this often to call all the 30-40 campus ministries together. This one really grew in attendance as there was a growing unity from the weekly "Leaders Prayer Meetings" we had started. We did the prayer meetings to give space for leaders of all groups a space to pray together and unite. We saw many come to the prayer meetings and their teams often came to these events for worship and prayer. It wasn't anything else but praise and prayer.

This poster is from the event that the kids from Temple Baptist Church where Dustin was youth minister came to UNC and did dramas on campus in 1996.

It was before Dustin, Daniel and Dan had the whole connection happen leading to Forest Fire, which took place that fall. Dan was possibly in attendance at this event. They attended this event and Dustin attended their Pit Praise and Praise nights without having a relationship.

The Temple youth came and preached, did dramas and prayed for campus revival. There were very few that attended which added to the shock when the actual Forest Fire event had thousands in attendance. If we were to judge attendance for the Forest Fire event that was to come by this event or any of the ICA events, we would have never dreamed as big as thousands.

The Daily Tar Heel from 1994 that finally listed Chi Alpha Omega as an actual Fraternity at UNC Chapel Hill.

After all of the many months of planning, recruiting and pestering the Dean of Student Affairs and his office, it was a dream to see this listing and I did not even know we had been accepted as a fraternal order by the school yet. They notified us after this posting in the paper.

Fraternity Shares Love Of Religion

BY SARAH YOUSSEF
STAFF WRITER

Carolina blue is not the only jersey color represented at UNC's women's basketball games. Every home game, without fail, a row of supporters donning royal blue and gold jerseys sits adjacent to the UNC bench.

They are the men of Chi Alpha Omega, the University's newest fraternity, and one of their main endeavors is supporting the Tar Heels' women basketball team.

"We want to cultivate Carolina pride and go out to support the women's basketball program," said Toby Scanlan, the fraternity's historian and treasurer. "We knew a couple of the players through Fellowship of Christian Athletes."

In fact, the idea to begin the Beta chapter of Chi Alpha Omega at Chapel Hill was conceived about one year ago at the 1994 NCAA Women's National Championship game.

Because it was Easter Sunday, some of the players asked a group of their supporters, who are now members of the fraternity, to lead a church service for the team.

"We were excited at the opportunity," said Dustin Hedrick, a sophomore from Statesville who is vice president and a founding member of the fraternity.

FRATERNITY
FROM PAGE 3

Overhearing the service was Tony Shanks, who chartered the original Chi Alpha Omega at East Carolina University in 1987. "Tony came up to us later and asked if we would be interested in starting a Christian fraternity at Carolina," Hedrick said. "I told him we were very interested."

Four months later, the group of nine original members assembled under fraternity. They participated in formal semester and gave out six bids.

"It was weird being on the ground floor... things and being responsible for a new organization, but that drew close together," said Randy Greene, a senior from C...

Greene said the founders are early members of campus groups, University Christian Fellowship of Christian Athletes, Campbell for Christ and Heels to H... Chi Alpha...

The Daily Tar Hill later did this piece on Chi Alpha Omega as word got out of our being an actual Christian Fraternity.

Our real purpose was to affect the other fraternities and sororities on campus by showing GOD's love as well as that it is possible to live for Christ and still be socially connected.

The newspaper wanted to focus more on the fact that we had supported the Women's Basketball program since they won the championship, so Dustin was mis-quoted in the paper, but we were happy for the press. We learned something about being in the papers. You have to be careful with what you say. They will cut many words into their thoughts. Fewer words control the media. Chi Alpha Omega was central in knowing Coach Hatchell.

130

Forest Fire was reported in Decision Magazine, (The Billy Graham Evangelical Association). Although they did not get all the details correct, it was such an honor to even be recognized by an organization that in our minds was led by a hero of our faith, Billy Graham.

Dustin had been involved with the Billy Graham crusades of the 1990's and had been featured in the Charlotte Observer at the event. He had worked with the counseling teams and was a avid supporter, driving from Chapel Hill to Charlotte and back nightly to be involved.

Dan had led the team at Forest Fire through the training that the BGEA used for their counselors. So, our counselors were trained in their method for the Forest Fire event.

To day that there was a great deal of respect for this organization is an understatement, so when they contacted us to report on the story, we were overwhelmed! Our 1997 version of viral media spread this story.

Carmichael auditorium is where we held Forest Fire 1997 and this is a picture from one of the many Women's Basketball games there. This is the court where Michael Jordan made his first collegiate slam dunk on NC State. It's also the place we spent tons of time with Chi Alpha Omega in support of Coach Hatchell and the team. That relationship set the stage for so much more in the future.

This is the "Prayer Closet" at the "Green House" Dustin built. This is after it had been painted and as he began to put names and prayer needs on the walls. This is place where the old ICA poster was taped on the wall and was prayed over. He traded his room for this closet and the couch, which is barely viewable beside the door above. This is the place where people would joke, "GOD is in his closet..." And is where people were saved as well as rededicated their lives.

THE TEMPLE BAPTIST YOUTH MINISTRY

The Temple youth group in action. I (Dustin) owe these kids much. It was in this precious community of young people that we encountered GOD and learned so much about what I now know about revival. I was blessed to walk with these passionate young people. The first picture above is from a lock-in event with the youth group. They were so hungry for revival that they loved prayer and ministry. I had planned a pizza party and capture the flag night and they asked to just pray all night for their lost friends and the church instead. This first picture was taken at about 1 or 2 am. They prayed for all of their friends and more to know Jesus and then they just waited on the LORD by praying , reading and encouraging each other. Soon after this picture, revival came to the church.

The second picture is from an outreach we did with our drama team. Every summer we went to the local trailer park for back yard Bible clubs, cookout, games and drama night. It was a week long event for the families. On the last night, we did a whole outdoor service with dramas and preaching and this night, we saw over 30 adults accept Jesus Christ after the dramas and we were able to grow the little church next door to the area by sending all the new converts there.

Kermit Harpold and his wife Becky spoke deeply into the work we were doing. He is a bi-vocational pastor in NC and owns a sign company called, "Signs and Wonders" and he was always planting churches.

His daughter Summer and I (Dustin) became friends while I was still in high school and I never knew that they would be so instrumental in deepening our lives in the Holy Spirit as well as helping me interpret

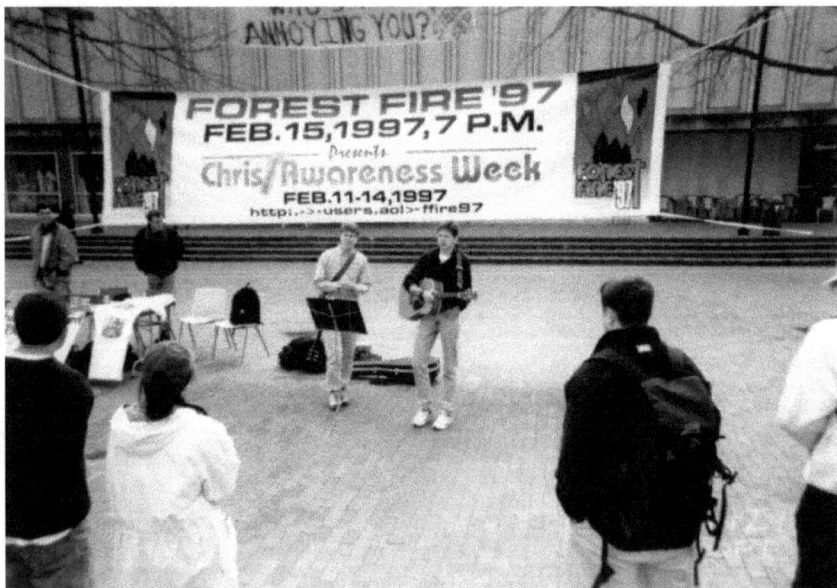

encounters I had in the closet.

Kermit made the banner for the event. The second picture is during the 1st day of what we called, "Christ Awareness week." We founded this week of demonstration in the Pit to precede Forest Fire 1997 so that all the lead teams from the 30-40 campus ministries could unit publicly on UNC campus and show their love for GOD and each other, they could stop and sing or preach and each group could sign up for a slot to lead during the week as their chance to share and lead. It was already our practice to spontaneously preach in the Pit as well as to have ICA "Pit Praise," but this was something more and gave the students access to the many groups in a very visible, public way and allowed the campus ministry members a very low cost way to introduce their friends to their faith and their community.

This is the only picture I have of the ICA Praise team or the event itself from the night of Forest Fire 97. We were just finishing up prayer and were preparing to go out to do the event. We had no idea how many people would be there when we walked out. It was so shocking to see the thousands of students that came that I forgot to take any more pictures. Who knew what was to come? Only GOD thinks it is a great idea to use the weak, small and the ones that have very little power as well as those that have no voice to do the greatest works in order that HE gets the most glory and no one can take credit.

Above you see one of the campus ministries' meetings the week after Forest Fire '97. The first meeting this group had during the 1993 fall semester did not fill this room at all which was just 3 years before. Now, look at the growth with overflow even in the balcony area. People had to stand around the edges and sit on the floor due to the sheer mass of attendance and there being too few seats. This was in the "Great Hall" at UNC. GOD was moving. And what we had prayed in during those years had stirred so much more. We had no idea in the beginning what the side effects would be in all of us.

We had purposely gone to other campus ministries' meetings before the event in order to pray for them, reach out to them and invite their leaders to meet with us in unity prayer meetings. Even the week prior to the meeting, we went to each campus ministry's meeting and asked to hand out flyers and communicate the event details to their group. So, we saw first hand how many were in the crowds. We went around afterwards to take pictures like this one and the one before and saw the after effects of the excitement on campus. What was truly exciting is many that were in these meetings now had not attended Forest Fire, the ones that attended had been so encouraged by the event, they invited their friends to their own campus ministry or group and therefore, there was this spreading of the excitement from person to person virally through relationship and we saw the literal growth for months afterwards till we all graduated. It was immense!

Above Daniel is leading worship at one of the events we did after FF'97. As the calls came in after the event, we were propelled into ministry as we shared the story of what had taken place and joined in with other colleges, universities, youth and student ministries to see the same happen where they were. At this event in Charlotte, NC, some of the UNC Charlotte students wanted GOD to move on their campus as well as in the youth in their area, so they had us come do a two-night youth event. Daniel and some of the ICA team led worship and I spoke. We only had about 20 youth the first night. We prayed through the night for GOD to move lost students to come with their friends as well as for the satanic strongholds against them to be broken. There were hundreds there the second night. At every event, the response after speaking was so large that we were unable to accommodate people coming forward for ministry at the front of the church or auditorium. Every time they would back up and kneel face down or prostrate weeping all the way down the aisles. This happened here and we were unable to move easily around to minister to those being saved.

At the end of the service which had gone well into the morning at this point, one young person came forward and asked that I come back and pray for the "gang" that they were a part of. The gang had come to be in opposition to the service, but as the end of the service came, they fell under heavy awareness of GOD's Presence and had gotten down under their pews in the very back, begging to be saved because they thought if they came forward, GOD would kill them. I went back to the back and looked under the pews and prayed for all of them as they wept and they asked Jesus into their hearts. The Father's love was powerful for conviction and repentance. This is something we need back. When GOD's Manifest Presence comes, people become aware of their sin, shame and pain as well as HIS greatness, beauty and healing. Only Holy Spirit can bring this kind of conviction. We must pray that HE does this again. You can stop right now and ask HIM, "Holy Spirit, in Jesus' name, please come on me in revelation of who Jesus and the Father are and make me aware of my shortcomings and shame. Come in my church and community and bring the gift of repentance back. Amen."

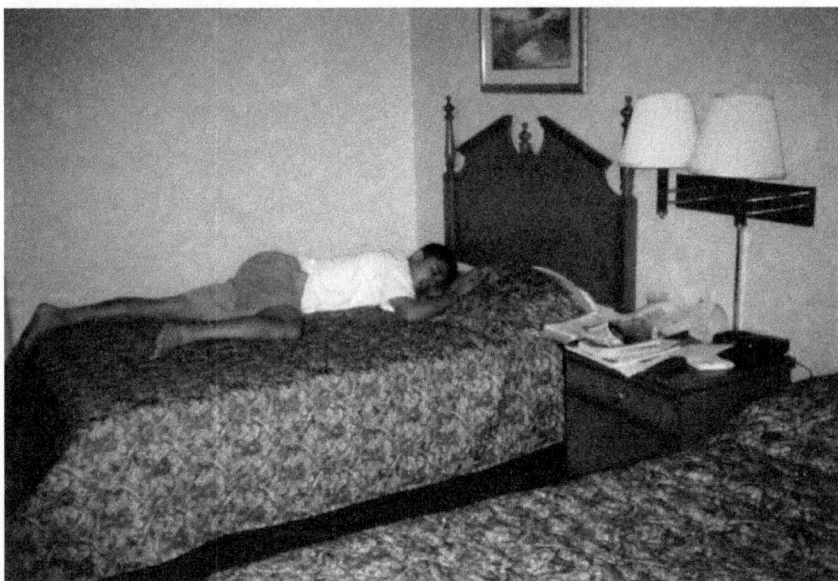

Above, this is Daniel as we were in our hotel room praying through the night at the Charlotte event in the last picture... well, almost. He made it to 7am.

We have always been serious about praying, fasting and breakthrough!

EMAILS FROM THE FOREST FIRE STORY

I am adding some of the emails to verify the effect of the story. We add these to stir you up and have marked out appropriate private information as needed.

To: DSHedrick@aol.com

Hey Dustin,

I got your message, but have no time this week!

I'm so glad that you had the opportunity to lead Forest Fire this year. And also, future thanks for coming to our campus which will happen! We are thinking about having a "student night" where people could come and give testimonies and of course you would be the main speaker. Pray for the right day and that other fellowships would get involved.

I agree that less movement is good for Sat. night, but you know how aching I am to tell people the "fire spark" story to others! :) So, I'll leave it up to you--but do remember the power of a student witness whether that be me, you, or Eugene.

Hmmm, I also wanted to tell you that there will be 15 from Longwood College attending, 20 from Elon, probably 15 from Davidson, and at least 40 from Wake forest. Don't worry, there will be more.

In Him,

Chad

Hi my name is Lori Johnson and I just wanted to let you know that I am coming to Forest Fire 97. I am excited about it and will continue to pray for this big event. If there is anything I can do please email me and let me know.

In His Love,
  Lori

Subj: Re: Fwd: edited email promo
To: DSHedrick@aol.com

Good luck with what you're doing, it sounds great!

I wish i could be there, so I just wanted to drop a silly line to say
that I support you.

Hope ev'thing goes well :)

-Nicole Capuano
 Boston College

Subject: Re: CAmpus Connection

Dear Dan,
Thanks so much for getting back to me with such encouraging words. I
like yo and have never met you .

Hey thought I would tell you I have an artist doing up some stuff for us
so what ever we can do to promote at Forrest Fire let me know, We are
trying to do all we canby word of mouth etc, to get word out about
Forrest Fire!

If you have names and address of people from the 16 Christian groups that
would be a great help. Thanks

Our goal is to have a venue for Christians but mostly we want to make the
gospel accessible to the lost in many different ways, for example we are
having concerts, like on MArch 16 Wed we have The Waiting doing a
concert
at Grace Church 200 Sage dr Chapel Hill NC>

We are also having the coffee house at least every other weekend and
sometime more often when we can book groups that fit the schedule and
our
goals.

I am planning a fun fun night for March 1 it is a take off of the Dave

Letterman show wit top ten list the works, Top 10 ways you know you are
in a bad church !! this is funny stuff plus we are doing much video
prodution stuff and have a herd hitting band to be the Paul Shaffer
equivelent. Synaxis for Raleigh. They are good too. Then they will end
the evening with a great concert. We will have the gospe in everything
we do some subtle and some in your face stuff like pit preaching and 2
question test booth are you going to heaven. But the coffee house and
production nights and the concerts will be low key inviting and
entertaining with different style bands that will attract a different
crowd from tme to time. We really want to be there to create a fishing
hole fro all Christian groups and area churches. I am sure word of mouth
will be our best advertisment .

Prayer is the work !! And we have many people doing that , we will
include yo in that as well.

How can we assist you ? Let me know we are the new kids on the block so
to speak but we are planning to do this right we actually have been on
campus 2 years but this was the semester we planned to go public in a big
way after much prayer and planning.

God Bless and keep in touch, we will have a news letter and mailing if
you would like to be on our list let me know , just send your email to me
and I will have DAwn add you to our mailing list.
See ya Doug Buehrle
><<><

Subj: Re: Praise the Lord!
To: dshedrick@aol.com

Dustin---

I know you will pray . . . so with faith in God I offer these requests.

Our Spiritual Emphasis Week begins on Sunday through Wednesday. It is an
annual revival that they hold here at Liberty every semester. The speaker
is Jay Strack. It is nightly beginning at seven pm. Pray for His presence
and that it will be a time where God is lifted up and He is worshipped. I
pray for spiritual eyes to be opened to the real battle that is at hand and
that no longer will we be lukewarm, but on fire for God!!!!!!!! Glory to Him!

Secondly, I already mentioned this to you in Charlotte, but once again I
feel burdened to ask you to pray. The dates for Atlanta, GA retreat is Feb.
27 to
March 1. Pray that God is the focus of everything.

I am praying for FF.

I believe,
sophia.

At 11:10 PM 1/27/97 -0500, you wrote:
>Sophia,
>
>Thanx so much for the info.
>
>You are in my prayers and I hope that the Lord will mightily use you at
>Liberty in the next few months. Just let me know if there is anything I
can
>do to help you see revival on your campus. For now, I pray.
>
>Lord Bless,
>Dustin

Subject: CAmpus Connection

Dear Dan,
I am Matthew Buehrle's dad and staff worker fro Campus Connection. We
are starting a Christian Venue and Coffee House on CAmpus and so excited
as we see all the CAmpus groiups working together. Our opening night is
Feb 1 in the Upendo Lounge . I just wanted to say I heard you all were
having Forest Fire so on that night we have canceled our Coffee House so
we can support what you all are doing there !! Thank you Lord!! I would
love the chance to set up a table in the entrance and advertise our
Coffee House if possible. We want to see something always happening on
campus and we do not want to water each other down so that is why I
canceled our night. I just want to support what you all are doing!! I
think I am repeating myself. now. If you think I could do some PR at
your event in a just being there sort of way let me know .
Your Brother In Christ,
Campus Connection Staff
Holy Grounds Coffee House

Doug Buehrle
Dave Rich
Thanks

Subj: Duke... Dan Elliott
To: DSHedrick@aol.com

Whoa Dustin...
Hmmmmm... Check this out!!!

Can we say, revival?

Dan

---------- Forwarded message ----------
Date: Mon, 27 Jan 1997 13:20:28 -0500 (EST)
From: Daniel Elliott <djelliot@acpub.duke.edu>
To: dantan@email.unc.edu
Subject: greetings...

Dan,

I apologize for not getting back to you until now. I am so happy that
the plans for Forest Fire came through and I rejoice in teh Lord's
provision, however it came about. I look forward to hearing from you
about how it all transpired. I also have quite a testimony to share, as
our normal 2 hour IV meeting went until 230 am on Friday noight as the
Lord brought aboiut a time of public confession and reconciliation. I
BELIEVE that the Lord is beginning a great and mighty work and I look
forward to it getting "too big for us to handle," as I remember you said
of Forest Fire. I just long for this stime to be completely in the hands
of God that we might just work as vessels for His grace to reach this
fallen world. I am so excited to have you guys on Friday, adn again the
Lord's work is perfect in having oyu guys come at the perfect ime. Oh, I
wish I could express my joy at seeing the Lord's fingerprints all over
this scheduling of events! He is so Awesome and worthy of our praise!!!

I hope to fill you all in completely on the details, bu tI think my

efficiency will be increased if I wiat to talk to you in person.
Hopefully I will call oyu tonight and we can chat, but it may be
difficult since we ar ecamping out for the bball game on Wed. I am still
hoping that you can come out to scout out our place and see what you guys
will have to do to set up. that would be best before Fri nioght so that
there will be no unexpected wrinkles. We must be faithful to prepare in
teh best ways we know how, right? I believe so. Good thing is that
God's grace and wisdom covers over all those things that we normally
forget to prepare, praise His name!! OK, I am outta here my man but look
forward to sharing some testimonies.......In His Service, Dan.

Bros and Sistas in Christ,

I am praising God that He is answering the prayer right now that I prayed
almost a year from now when I suffered from a chronic Elijah complex
(feeling alone in my walk with God) and prayed that He would just open up
so many opportunities for me to meet people of God that I would hardly be
able to receive them and what can I say? Nothing but God is so good and
each day I meet more people who introduce me to more people so that I
really don't have to do anything but stand back and say "praise

God"...(Holy Spirit just said that's the way it should have been all
along, huh?...yeah, that's about right)...

well, Jocelyn Jones, a leader in organizing Unity and Harmony 2000-A
Conference on Racial Reconciliation wants to meet with all Christian
campus leaders, student organizers, and people of God interested in this
event in a meeting tentatively scheduled for 6 p.m. on Friday, February 7.
I pray that as many as possible of you will be able to attend. She wants
to meet all of you and talk to you in person as well as answer any
questions, get feedback, etc. She can better explain than I can about
things and her phone number is (919) 851-8823. Also, another leader on
the planning committee of this event, Mrs. Dawson can be reached at (919)
787-6787. I am going to call her tomorrow actually to try and see if I
can drive to Raleigh soon to pick up some more flyers and letters about
the event. If any of you are wondering how I know you, which is a
legitimate concern...many of you, I do not know personally but Dan from In
Christ Alone at UNC-Ch put me on his Christian leaders listserve and I
guess I just trusted the Lord that everything would be O.K...hope so

Dan also asked me to remind people that Forest Fire '97 is still looking
for counselors who are willing to go through witness training in order to
really be there for the people that we are trusting in faith that the Holy
Spirit will lead to rededicate themselves to or accept for the first time
Jesus Christ. If you have any questions e-mail Dan at
dantan@email.unc.edu. They really despearately need counselors,
volunteers, ushers, and help in general from us to bring people to Christ.
The Forest Fire web-site is at http://users.aol.com/ffire97 for more info.
Also, in the spirit of all of the awareness weeks that this campus
has...domestic violence awareness week, race relations awareness week,
Dan
and I just discussed tonight during the week of February 10-14 during
which they Pit at our lovely campus, UNC, is reserved for godly activities
to have a Christ Awareness Week and Speak-Out. This forum could bring
Christians all over this campus as well as pastors from the Chapel
Hill/Durham area together. We need to know who each other are as Dan
and
I (as well as other believers on thecampus noticed) that a prevelent
spriti of fear permeates this campus...which we know is not of God (II
Timothy 1:7-8). So many people have remarked to me, Dan, amnd probably

to
you all as well that they feel alone in their walk with the Lord on this
very campus and I know some people who are scared of the condemnation
of
the world to profess Christ. By coming together with all of our
denominations, backgrounds, ministries, etc. as the Body of Christ we can
provide a powerful testimony and big-time annointing that makes
unbelievers so jealous of our love for each other through Christ that they
just HAVE to confess that Jesus is Lord. If people don't want to do this,
of course, it won't fly...put if after praying about it, you feel that
this would be something that you would want to find out more about doing
and organizing please call me (Talya) at 914-2682 or e-mail Dan at
dantan@email.unc.edu (I don't like to give other people's phone numbers
out unless they say it's O.K. beforehand). Since we have the Pit for Feb.
10-14, it would take all of our faith put in action and telling a lot of
people in ministries and people in general to make this happen. Envision
people our age talking to each other about Jesus...yes, it can happen with
God on this campus...

that's all...sorry so long...

I'll be praying for each and every one of you.

your sis in Christ

Talya

Friends,

I just recieved this great e-mail and thought that each of you would relate to it.

I hope that each of you are doing well and I hope to see each of you in the next few weeks.

In the light,
Zac

To: DSHedrick@aol.com
Date: 97-02-20 10:35:06 EST

Dustin,

        What a blessing and encouragement was your note. Praise God. We
are in New Hampshire, and I am sending your note on to about 100 pastors
up here to encourage them. If any of you come north, please come to our
church here and give your testimonies about what God is doing there. We
want the fire to come to New England. Myself and 6 other pastors are
going to Brownsville the first week in March.

        Keep us informed. I am going to put your letter on our bulletin
board.
Oden L. (Bud) Woodward
Chichester Congregational Church
153 Main Street, Chichester, NH 03234-6512
King of Kings, Lord of Lords...Christ Jesus, the same yesterday, today,
and forever
Working together, to build the kingdom of God!

To: DSHedrick@aol.com
Date: 97-02-20 09:44:58 EST

Dustin,

Thank you so much for your report about Forest Fire 97. I am a
professor at a college here in the northwest. We experienced the wave
of campus revivals two years ago that began in Texas. Do you think a
new wave of campus revivals is beginning?

We are very interested, and praying for you and the schools who are
being touched.

Larry Asplund
Portland Bible College
Portland, Oregon

Forwarded message:
Subj: Forest Fire
Date: 97-02-20 16:30:30 EST
From: Jizex
To: DSHedrick

Dear Dustin:
My name is James Isaacs, I am a doctoral student in music at USC in Los
Angeles, Ca. I was inspired by your letter to Richard Riss on what you're
doing in N. Carolina.

I've been to Toronto also and have been in the river for almost 3 years. I'm
thinking that I should start a prayer meeting with all the Christian groups
on campus to pray together for revival.

A number of people at my church, Harvest Rock Church in Pasadena have been
fasting and praying for revival during Lent of this year. Do you know of
Bill Bright's book called "The Coming Revival"?

It's coming! We haven't seen anything yet!!!

Let me know if you have any ideas as to how I could get this started. It
just occured to me to ask the Campus Crusade for Christ people.

I'll be keeping you in my prayers.

Blessings

James Isaacs

From: dkim@unccvx.uncc.edu
To: ghoonkim@email.unc.edu, ptl@email.unc.edu, eklee@unity.ncsu.edu,
DSHedrick@aol.com, gmccg@bellsouth.net, sschun@liberty.edu
Date: 97-02-20 23:46:23 EST

Brothers and sisters,

Our God is an awesome God!!!

As most of you already know, God has put great burden
on me to pray for UNCC!! Well, God is working. He
is always at work. (Blackaby and King)

It all started when I approached this christian brother
after my marketing class to tell him about FFIRE97!!!
We talked ... and God did the rest. He and ten others
went to FFIRE97!! Praise God!!! Wait, I haven't got
to the really good news yet...

After I talked to this brother, I went to my next class.
For some reason, God started to stir my heart with visions
for revival at UNCC!!! I did not want just rely on my feelings,
so I started to pray..... ah yeah baby !!!

Two weeks have past since then and still God kept bugging me
about UNCC!! He eventually led me back to that christian brother
to share with him God's visions for our school.

I called him... we praised God... and then I asked Brad
to pray. Man! This guy had so much FIRE in his heart.
He reminds me of Dustin!!

Brothers and sisters, Brad and fellowship and I will be
praying on our own until Tuesday of next week. I will also be
meeting Brad @ Tuesday 4-6 PM to talk about God's plans.
God will lead us from there!!!!

I urge you to keep Charlotte in your prayers. I don't
know details. As always, God is only showing me what's
in front of my feet. I will let you know more when God
shows me more. Please keep praying.

Why pray? Because I want you to ask God if He wants you
to be part of His work in any way. If he does want you

to work and you don't ... God will burn your butt for
not responding to His intiative!!!

Please forward this message to all those who you think will
pray for this event.... I will keep all of you updated.

<><
yd

158

Dustin,

My name is Ryan Purtell. I am a Senior at Texas A&M University. I recently read a copy of your e-mail about what God is doing on the college campuses in North Carolina. It was sent to me by a friend, and I have no idea how he got it.

It is so wonderful to hear that God is moving on other college campuses around the country. Ever since revival has began to spread across the United States, many have felt that the colleges and universities would eventually become hot-beds for Christian growth. The vision of these people is definitley comming to pass.

God is doing great things here at Texas A&M. We have a weekly bible study that draws around 3,000 college students weekly. It is called Breakaway, and is heald at Central Baptist Church in Bryan on Tuesday nights. What is so amazing is to see such a large number of Texas Christians who come and really worship Jesus. Texas churches have been plagued by a certain stoicism and legalism over the past few decades. God is showing, once again, that he can overcome. Enrollment in every major Christian orgainzation on campus has reached its record high.

Well I have to run to my Logic class (unfortunately). I would love to hear more from you about what God is doing in North Carolina. Got to run. God bless.

,Ryan   Purtell
Class of 97'

Dear Dustin,

You wrote:

--snip--

Though professors, this world and our peers may pour water over our wood,
our God is the God who burns wet wood! (See 1Kings 18:30-39).

I pray that God continues to spread the fire to our college campuses. As for
now, I pray for more!

Thanks so much for all of the encouragement,

God bless,
Dustin Hedrick
DSHedrick@aol.com

--snip--

I for one am a professor who is praying for the fire to come down! I think one should be praying for faculty and other students instead of cursing them. No condemnation, brother...I just spent a day on campus with the Father telling me over and over and over how He loves each one so
passionately!

God has His agents in all areas of life, even university faculty...well, He is just that awesome!

I am really VERY excited about FOREST FIRE's activities...any chance you all could visit the University of Hawaii?

I pray for a greater release of the Holy Spirit's power and passion for Jesus in and through you and your colleagues! Zap Dustin now Father! Let him be a lightning rod of Your glory...

Blessings on you....:)

Jeffrey C. Ady, Ph.D.
Assistant Professor and Chair, Graduate Studies
Department of Communication
University of Hawaii at Manoa

Whew....can somebody say Praise the Lord!!! Say it agian...Praise the Lord!!!!! Hallelujah.....I just want to share with taht JESUS IS REAL!!! He is really real to me.....Praise the Lord.....God is so good....wow halleluhya.......

The reason I am so excited is because my Father is restoring my Joy!!!! The Bible details in Nehemiah that the Joy of the Lord is your strength....Yes, that's right....the joy of the Lord is your strength....

Gang....let me talk to you for a second......I went to a conference down in the heartland of North Carolina...in to the Jaws of the Ram this weekend (Carolina)....it was called Forest Fire...and boy did it set a blaze in my heart...not only that but God really poured out His Spirit at what seemed like to me the most inopportune times....but for Him (and me) itwas perfect timing.....Praise Him!!!! Anyway....We heard a young man, whose name some might know (Clayton King), and He reminded us about seeking first the kingdom of God.....seeking first the Kingdom of God....yall do you realize when you seek first the Kingdom ofGod and all His righteous that you don't have to worry about a single thing....why because it is God who gives the increase in everything....He promises in Deut. 8:6....that if we would just simply walk in His ways and obey that we will have properity in this lifetime....and gang, I am not talking about blab it and grab.....or even name it claim...I am talking about having everything that you need and desire....for the word of God says in II Corinthians 9:8---that God is able to make all grace abound to you that at all times in all things having all that you need you will about in every good work....." It is just that simple.....let your passion be for Christ and let it be renewed.....Yall God is on themove and He is passionately wanting us tot jump on His bandwagon and ride with Him.....Do you realize that God really wants to work with you in the areas of ministry....Do you realize that the gifts and callings of God are

Subject: dinky is trying ...

Brothers and sisters,

This message is not to focus on that dinky satan...I am
sharing this with you to give encouragement and glorify
OUR LORD!!!!!! I can't wait any longer...I want to see
God rock that campus UP SIDE DOWN....

As of now, there are 13 people coming up from Charlotte
for FFIRE97!!

Everything was ready. I was going to leave for Chapel Hill
early in the morning...David and Nancy (ah ji mah) were supposed
to drive up in their cars around noon. All 3 cars were going
to be packed. No room to breathe... oh no.. stinky kim chi breathe!

Plans changed ... David calls me today and tells me that his car
broke down and that he won't able to pick up people...
This is a BIG, BIG PROBLEM!!!
My heart started to feel heavy... but I knew this was

the work of satan... so I started to pray..
I called others and told them to pray.. aaahhh yeah :)

Prayer answered!! The phone rang.. It was Nancy "ah ji ma".

I really did not want to discourage her with bad news...
but before I could tell her ... she told me that her husband
told her to rent a van because he was scared
for the kids safety...(nancy's car is old). This is all God!!!

God is in total control!!! -- main point of this story!

Praise God. Trust in the Lord!!!!

Man, I feel so rebuked. I am nothing. He is EVERYTHING!!!

God answered prayer in less than 10 minutes!!!

Now, I know this might be "nothing" to most of you, but to
me this is a great big miracle. Why, you ask?

I really feel satan did not want certain people to go.
- kids like FRANCES and david's sister, MARY. There are
others, but these two you know.. Especially FRANCES..
(Susan is not coming. Just FRANCES!)

May God do His mighty long awaited work... For all we
know, God could have planned FFIRE97!! just for these
two.

I really believe.

∝
yd

From: Brianwandr
Subj: Re: FWD: Forest Fire 97
To: DSHedrick

Read your testimony. God bless you in your passion for Him and your
desire to see youth saved!

"Lord, let Your power fall on this man in Jesus' name. Power to heal the
sick and the broken. Power to cast out demons. Power to speak the Word
of God with boldness. Power to tear down strongholds in the minds of
unbelievers. Unleash him and his whole team to do Your mighty works.
Amen."

Brian Andrews

To: DSHedrick@aol.com

I read your message that was posted to the Awakening Listserv, and got really excited because we are just beginning to do worship here at Valparaiso University. We are a private, Lutheran affiliated university of about 3500 students. I attend the Vineyard Christian Fellowship here in 'Valpo' and also work here. We have done one worship night with about 50 attending, but the reaction was so positive that we are moving to a bigger room and hope to get over 100 next time. Please pray that a 'forest fire' of the Spirit would start and spread here!
In the love of Christ,

David Fevig
Director of Financial Aid
Valparaiso University

Dustin,

Praise the LORD brother!!!!! Saturday was awesome!! You have already taught me a lot in the short time we have known each other.

Are you still going to pray with ICA on Tuesdays?

I hope you got a lot of rest this weekend--you deserve it.

Kristen

Dustin, I thought the conference went really well. We brought another couple
from our church, and we all were greatly impressed with the response you received and the amount of interest we saw.

I pray that this will only be the beginning of great things to happen at UNC.

If I can be of service to you in any way, please let me know. We are greatly
encouraged and feel more than ever that it is extremely important that the
churches of this community support the "remnant" that is on campus.

YOU TOO ARE A WARRIOR...SO FIGHT THE GOOD FIGHT OF FAITH....GOD WILL SOON
REWARD YOU....

PRAY FOR ME.....THAT I WOULD BE EVER PASSIONATE ABOUT THE NAME AND THE
GOSPEL OF CHRIST JESUS, MY SAVIOR, AND LORD.

"YOU CAN DO ALL THINGS THROUGH CHRIST"

THE PEOPLE WHO KNOW THEIR GOD WILL DO EXPLOITS...

ERIC

PS there will soon be a websit up from me so be looking for it....
right now it's underconstruction.....but it will be

irrevocable....YOu guys listen, God is calling us out of this
insignificant mode some of us have gotten ourselves into and He is
callingn ALL of us to be TEAM players.....yes, He is.......He really is
and He is doing all that Can for us....Here me please, Joel talks about
God pouring out His Spirit all flesh....Yes, that means you, me, Sally
SUe, and buffy too......No one is to be left out....WE all that ability in
Christ to minister and He is calling us to the Purpose of Being a people
of Passion....no more of this half-hearted Christianity that comes from
our lips and not our heart.....Ask yourself are you truly living the way
Jesus did....These are serious times and we are people of a Joyful, free,
funloving, but also a serious God...for He serous about the souls of
men and women and the condition of their hearts.......He has called us to
intercession, He has also called us to prayer, He has called us to take
thte Kingdom of darkness by force and snatch people from flames
hell...No it is done by His Spirit and we know what Zech. 4:6 tells us
that it is not by Might nor Power, but by the Spirit of the Lord..wow...BE
encouraged Gang
that you have the ability to minister in the Spirit...Why? Because you
are a Spirit being......if you the Holy Spirit dwelling within you then
you have the abililty from heaven to minister...no matter where you may
be.....at home, at work, on the playground.....WE need to be forceful in
taking the Kingdom.....WE are not of those who shrink back and are
destroyed, but who are forceful in taking the Kindgom...and you know what
the devil would come to you even know and put doubt and fear in your
about
doing what God has called you to do....but we know that Paul told Timothy:

"For God has not given us a Spirit of fear, but of power,
of love, and of a sound mind." II Tim 1:7

Yall, God has given us a Spirit of Power....for the Kingdom of God is not
a matter of talk, but a matter of Power.....let us not talk the kingdom of
God, but lets walk in it with Power....with Power!!!! God has given us a
Spirit of Love....for He Himself is love....and the fruit of the Spirit is
love.......and He has given us a sound mind (the Mind of Christ)....No
worry you have been given the heavenly ability through the empowerment
(baptism) of the Spirit to do the work of God along side God...He will
accompany you.....so be encouraged God wants you to seek first His
Kingdom and He will make the way for you....Don't worry about the money

Date: 97-02-20 10:09:20 EST

Dustin,

Your inspirational message was forwarded to me, but many sentences in the paragraphs were somehow missing.

Dustin, my precious son, Austin, had gone twice to Toronto where his life was radically changed; he found the power of God for repentance and ministry there. Sadly, one year ago tomorrow, his beautiful life was snuffed out by a drunk driver. Austin, 22, was on his way to work; he had just left his fiancee's house. On Saturday, we will plant a cross in his memory near the scene of his death.

As a result of the renewal in Austin's life, my father (who served as a deacon in a Southern Baptist Church for 40 years), my mother, my Catholic Aunt and Uncle, many cousins, our other three children and my wife and I have found new life in our Christian walk! We are now attending Shady Grove Church (was Southern Baptist until the Convention kicked it out in the mid 70s because the pastor dared to pray for sick, anointing them with oil, etc.) where our lives continue to grow in Christ. To make a long story short, many people have been saved and lives renewed with the "planting" of the seed of our son. Please check out the homepage dedicated to his memory; the URL is:http://abacus.mwsu.edu:5000/~land/.

By the way, Austin and his siblings grew up in Abidjan, Cote D'Ivoire (French West Africa) where we served 15 years as Southern Baptist foreign missionaries. I am now professor of journalism at the University of North Texas, Denton TX near Dallas.

Another note, our son, Drew Land, 22, leads worship at one of our churches near Dallas and his involved in a Holy Spirit led firestorm of a revival on THIS campus..... one of our "sister" churches, which was formerly Church of Christ, has established a cell of college students (my son helps lead worship there) that has grown to 35 just since January, with 8 salvations and last night Drew came home glowing, rejoicing, walking on air because of the power of God in that meeting!

Please sign the guestbook at Austin's homepage. And please re-send

me your testimony.

God bless you in your walk!

Mitch Land

169

To: DSHedrick@aol.com (Dustin Hedrick)
Date: 97-02-21 01:09:07 EST

This is in regards to Liberty Forest Fire.

gk <><

---------- Forwarded message ----------
Date: Wed, 19 Feb 1997 17:10:48 -0500
From: Sophia Chun <sschun@liberty.edu>
To: Chi-hun Kim <ghoonkim@email.unc.edu>

Oppa,

I talked to the Vice President of Spiritual Affairs.
His name is Pastor Rob Jackson. I told him about
Forest Fire last Sat. He said that he had heard good
things about it . So, he knew what
I was talking about. Anyways, I asked him what he would
think if we brought it to Liberty and he said that it
would be a good idea, except he didn't think that it would
happen this semester. He is leaving for India on Saturday of
this week and will not return until March 7. Then during
Spring Break he is leaving for another place. He said
time wise the spring semester is booked up and he is the only
person who can give the OK for an event like this.

He said that possibly next semester it was possible. He asked
about the vision behind it and so I told him everything. He
seemed to be interested. He said another problem with bringing
in a group from outside our school is that the Campus Pastor's
office would have to bring them in since they are not affiliated
with a club on campus. If the CP's office brings them in then
he has the responsibility to check out all the politics like
doctrinal statement and denomination stuff. He asked who the past
speaker was and he knew of Clayton King because of India and World Help.

I told him that I just wanted to see if there was a possibility

for this semester and that confirmation from God was not yet sure.
He said that as he saw it, it was not possible this semester, but he
said that if you wanted to continue to pray about it and you were sure
that God was in it, than for you to contact him and talk with him
personally.

Ok. If there is anything else that I can do let me know.

sophia.

Date: Monday, January 27, 1997 3:09:16 AM
From: ghoonkim@email.unc.edu (Chi-hun Kim)
Subj: OPPA!!!!!! (fwd)
To: DSHedrick@aol.com, JLin7@aol.com, dantan@email.unc.edu

Just thought a part of this email would encorage you guys...

read on..

---------- Forwarded message ----------
Date: Sun, 26 Jan 1997 20:37:32 -0500 (EST)
From: YASHI121@aol.com
To: ghoonkim@email.unc.edu
Subject: OPPA!!!!!!

sup oppa...
so how was everything...the revival...
i hope it went very well...

the Packers are creaming the Patriots rite now...oh yeah...
it's 27 to 14...
if u can't tell...i am a cheesehead...
i don't know jack about the rules of football...
but i just like the Packers because they're from Wisconsin...
that's weird...of all states...to see a Pro football league in Wisconsin...

i had this weird dream about UNC...
i don't know why i dreamt about UNC...
my friends and family were at UNC for some really big event...
i don't know what event...
but there were thousands of people there...

they were on the bleachers and on the field...
maybe i was dreaming about that thing at UNC in February...
the revival...
i don't know...but it was strange...

well i hope u are doing spiff...
i hope to get that pic. of u in the Big Apple soon...

well talk to u later oppa! :-)
Hannah....

DeDustin,

BBrother...I can't tell you how much you blessed me today....It was such a blessing to see you and the sensitivity. that God has placed within you....I can see how much maturity that God has been doing with you...and to have such a kindred spirit with someone is so refreshing to me since I am used to meeting people all the time....and lately as I was telling Summer I have not really met any body really fresh lately....and you were a breath of fresh to me today....really....I don't want to fill you head with a lot of flattery....but I want to tell you to continue in your perserverance in the Lord.....for you are getting ready (and already have) touched a lot of people....I can just tell it.....like one thing I noticed was like you were not always trying to get the spotlike and that you really enjoy the background....and I have been learning that those who choose to be in the background God likes to move forward...into the light...for the scriptures tell us that those things done in secret (good or bad) will be revealed in the open.....this means prayers.....actions...attitudes....and other aspects that we never talk about or thought about....the Word of God covers all aspects of our lives....Hey brother I want you to know that I am expecting great things from you.....God is going to use you to touch thousands...and maybe even to cross denominational and racial barriers...God is going to use you... even in ministry to children....I am so blessed to know you.....praise God....There is so much in store Dustin.....so much......I feel the Lord telling me to tell you to continue into intercession that is going to be a place of power for you....a tremendous place of power.....you will begin to see the results of your prayers soon...don't worry about your family.... friends...finances....why because God is going to take care of you....yes He is .....Praise Him...allajdfklajfklajfdakljfkaljfakjfklajflk anyway brother keep in touch...and I will be glad to talk with you and

pray for you.....so keep in touch......The Battle is mine says the Lord.

Eric

172

From: RGreene563
Subj: You think you are so cute!
To: DSHedrick

What do you mean progressed to the world of AOL, pretty soon I am going to surpass you and be a Netscape Navigator. :)
     Bobby is coming to Forest Fire. I really believe that this is going to be an awesome revival that can touch other campuses besides UNC. I pray for revival here and there daily and that forest fire will be a tool for that revival. God is awesome!

In Him,
Randy

Subj: Re: God is so good!!!!
Date: Mon, Feb 3, 1997 11:12 AM EDT
From: dkim@unccvx.uncc.edu
To: DSHedrick@aol.com

Dustin,

Yes, God is so good!!!

He has started a prayer group on Sundays after our worship
service. The group right now consists of me, David, Becky,
Tony and Charles. Man, they are hungry!!!!! We can't wait
who God is going to bring in next. We believe. All of us
are just in awe of God's gripping grace!!!

Right now, I am personally praying for Frances. I don't know
why, but God just told me to. So I am.

Dustin, God is at work and we are experiencing His blessing.
This is not an understatement!!! Just wait till the next
update.

For now, we are excited about FFire97! We are praying.

Praise God. I worship Him alone.

I know now what it means to believe in God!

ᗢ<
Daniel
See you soon.

From: sh25037@appstate.edu
X-From: sh25037@appstate.edu (Bon Bon)
To: DSHedrick@aol.com

Dustin,
Hi! I just wanted to thank you again for coming up this weekend! I had an
Awesome time, and I am so glad that you finally got to meet all my new
friends. I just want you to know that everyone just loves you to death up
here. They all feel like they have known you forever, and they are
constantly asking me if you are going to come back up. I told them you
wanted to come up after Forest Fire, and Darrell wanted me to ask you if
you
would do another skit with us while you were here. He told me last night
at
New Life that he knew that you were a Man of God, and that God had an
awesome plan for your life. He said that he could just see God so strong
in
your life, and that you had a major anointing on your life. He also told me
that he could see you coming up and helping him speak at different places,
and at new life. HELLO!!!! Eric says that he feels like you all have known
each other forever! He really wants to get to know you better, just like
everyone else! :) I am not sure if you have heard from Jeff or not, but be
praying for him. Tonight at leadership meeting, I could tell he was really
down. I think that part of it is the Michelle deal. He really wants to ask
her out, but he isn't sure if that is what God wants him to do. I haven't
had a chance to get to talk to him after the meeting, but I will see him
tomorrow at morning prayer. It might help if you could write or talk to
him
if you get a chance. He could use the encouragement! He told me that
anytime you wanted to come back up, you were welcome to stay with him.
I
think it is so unreal how God placed relationships in your life with people
from here. I am so excited to see what God has instore! Well, it isn't
long to Forest Fire. How are things going? I am praying hard for
everything, and especially you. YOU need a refreshing, and I know God is

going to take care of you and all your needs. :) I miss you already, and I
hope to hear from you soon! Talk to you soon! Call if you get a spare
moment (YEA right!). God bless you!!!!

Love in Christ,
Summer :)

ps .... the return address says bon bon and that is because I am in
Bonnie's room!:) Philemon 4: "I always thank my God as I remember you in
my
prayers!"
Bonnie

Date: Tue, 4 Feb 1997 16:05:37 -0500 (EST)
From: GOD IS GOOD ALL THE TIME <chriskim@wam.umd.edu>
To: Chi-hun Kim <ghoonkim@EMAIL.UNC.EDU>
Subject: Re: FEB 15

Whats up Ghoon hyung, how are things? SOrry about not coming down before
school started, things kinda got hectic. Anyways, I have checked out the
web site, pretty cool, I got to get one of those cool t-shirts! I really
want to come down for this, even Hyun Jung nu-na has been asking me and
Sue to come down. I'll to CJ and see if the college group could go
together or something, but I really don't want to miss this and it also
gives me a chance to see my bro at UNC! GOD IS GOOD AND FAITHFUL for
breaking down all those obstacles that this rally faced, I will continue
to pray for this rally and for everyone involved, espc. you and Hyun Jung

nu-na. Man you must have been real busy these days mr.coordinator. I'll
try to call you within the next couple of days and I'll write back asap.
Talk to you later hyung, and as always PRAISE THE LORD!!!!!!

Your little bro,
Chris

Subj: Re: new prayer coordinator
Date: Fri, Feb 7, 1997 3:13 AM EDT
From: ica@listserv.oit.unc.edu
X-From: dantan@email.unc.edu (Daniel Tan)
Sender: owner-ica@listserv.oit.unc.edu
Reply-to: ica@listserv.oit.unc.edu
To: ica@listserv.oit.unc.edu (In Christ Alone)

A volunteer who will be one of our counselors called me to let me know
that there will be a prayer meeting on Wednesday's at 3:00pm in the Union
to pray for the campus.

Please spread the word for anyone who has the heart!

Dan

To: JLin7@aol.com

greetings in the name of Christ!

my name is david yum, and I am the contact person for Forest Fire at
Davidson College.
First, praise God for all the work He has done in preparing the night!
Second, praise Him for instilling in you guys the drive and motivation
to put it together. I really look forward to it after going to FF '96.

I expect to bring anywhere between 5-7 people from Davidson, and our
transportation is set.

i guess i'll see ya saturday!

in Him,
david Yum

Subj: Pit Praise!
Date: Tue, Feb 11, 1997 3:39 PM EDT
From: ica@listserv.oit.unc.edu
X-From: kapark@eos.ncsu.edu
Sender: owner-ica@listserv.oit.unc.edu
Reply-to: ica@listserv.oit.unc.edu
To: ica@listserv.oit.unc.edu

Hi ICA

The pit praise was so awesome today!!!!!
That was my first time to pit praise
and also to any outdoor praise I have ever had.
It was most awesome feeling I experienced.

Sometimes when I walk on campus just whispering doesn't
fill me up. It's like there is something inside that
wants to come out..... not just during worship and praise time.
You just want to worship and praise Him without thinking about
where you are and whom you are with.
I had that opportunity today at UNC campus!
I just couldn't believe myself being out there in the middle
of campus, just praising God. WOWWWW!!!!!
It was too good to be true!
The weather was so cold but the sun was shining right through
us, to OUR SPIRIT! What a wonderful God!
It was cold outside but it was God who kept us hot inside!!!
I was having so great time out there with God today.
And I am even more excite for Forest Fire!
If I was excited for what God had done today I am sure
we all going to be amaze for what God is going to do on Feb 15!

PTL!!!!!!!

Kyung Ah

Subject: RE: power of prayer

Brother,

This is great encouragement for me...

I pray that God will bless ICA for it's faith
in prayer....

God has been really leading me to pray

more sincerely for those who are coming
up for forest fire...

Currently, there are 8 kids from my youth
group who are going to be there...God will
bless them. I know. I trust in the Lord!

There are also two other brothers in my mktg class..
I will see them today. I should get answer on
whether they and their fellowship will go
to forest fire... Brother and sisters,
I just want you to know that more revival
is yet to come. Just watch and be amazed ..
The HAND OF GOD has much blessing to do!!!

To all my brothers and sisters in ICA...
Be unified this week .. in the Mighty Name
of Jesus. Prayer is definitely lifted up
your way!!!

Yes, brother G-Hoon. There is definitely
Power of Prayer present in the campus of
North Carolina!!!! God has to be pleased.

- - - -

Hyung, please forward to all you think
needs it. I am getting more and more
people to pray for FFIRE!!

✂
yd

Dear Dustin,

Thank you for your message! Our summer break is from May 12 to August 26,
which is the first day of classes. My guess is that the second or third week of classes would be best as things simmer down here...

The congregation to which I belong ["My Father's House"] is currently is a period of prayer and fasting...I will add this to our prayer agenda.

Give Dustin et al. more, Lord!!! You're the God of no limits...the God of NOW...the God Who is too much! Pour it on...crank it up!!

Yours,

Jeff

Hey Dustin,

It's me from Oklahoma, or should I say Howdy Dustin!!!(Ha Ha Ha)

It started raining on Thursday so my family and I decided to head back
home.
We ran into some really bad storms on the way too. We only got to
Arkansas,
so we spent the night there. I hope you remember who I am!? Just in case
you don't, you met me in line at Brownsville!!

I just got home at about 6:00p.m. today. And I thought I would just write
and say I really enjoyed talking to you and Randy and I totally forgot the
other guys name. What was it? (Don't tell him I forgot his name, I would
feel bad if he knew!!) Tell Randy that the Okie said Howdy. And the other
guy too.

E-mail me back soon. I would write more but I am dead tired so I am fixin'
(okie talk) to go to bed!!!!

If you are ever in Oklahoma give me a call and maybe you can come and
speak
in church or on a youth night. My dad would love for you to. (918)
287-4070

Kristin Swafford

Dustin Hedrick
Forest Fire 97
624 W. Lackey Farm Road
Stony Point, NC 28678

Dear Dustin,

Please accept this small gift to help you cover the cost of Forest Fire 97. May God continue to pour out his blessing on your work.

Seeking the Glory of King Jesus,

Chris and Holly Johnson

Dustin-

My name is Heather Sawyer and I am a student leader of a ministry on the
campus of Louisiana State University. A friend of mine forwarded a letter to
me that you had sent to Richard Riss regarding the Forest Fire Conference and
the move of God on the campuses of North Carolina. I also came out of the
Southern Baptist Convention and was touched by God in a new way about 5 years
ago. Now I work with a multi-denomenational group sponsored by my church.

When I first came to LSU, the Lord gave me a vision similar to what you
described in your letter. Like never before, the ministries on our campus are
beginning to unify and pray for revival. Every leader of every organization
had described having a similar vision for having a praise fest of some type
on our campus. I am convinced like never before that God wants to do a
powerful work on our campuses and in our generation. I just want to thank
you for your letter; it has renewed my vision. (sometimes you can get so
bogged down in "ministry" that you can lose your vision). Also, if there is
any information you could send me about Forest Fire '98 I would greatly
appreciate it. Again, thanks so much and be blessed!!

On fire-
Heather Sawyer
President, Destiny Campus Ministries, LSU

REVIVAL TIMELINE AND JOURNALS FROM UNC

I am adding my revival timeline that I started and kept through my time at UNC. It literally is a response to what Dr. Henry Blackaby told me to do and that was to study the revivals and movements of GOD in history. I am also adding some of my journals and thoughts from back then so they are here for you to see some of the maturing and immaturity of my thoughts. Again, we did NOT have it all together nor were we the popular crowd. We simply had obedience and passion. GOD did the rest.

These are here for encouragement and reference. My challenge to you is to begin to write down everything GOD is showing you as you attempt our divine experiment together and just see what happens. I cannot wait to see what GOD does even greater through you than me.

Reviewer: Anon

Keyword   : J.H.Merle D'Aubigne

ATLA RELIGION DATABASE 1996

   Year: 1846   Type: Review (Beth)

   Author: Merle d'Aubigne, Jean H
    Title: Discourses and Essays of the Rev J H Merle D'Aubigne; tr by
           Charles W Baird
   Journal: Methodist Review 28:480 Jl 1846
    Pages: 466

Imprint: New York: Harper, 1846

Journals: Methodist Review

Reviewer: Anon

Keyword   : Adolphe Monod

ATLA RELIGION DATABASE 1996

   Year: 1985   Type: Review

   Author: Deen, James L
    Title: Prophet and Peacemaker: The Life of Adolphe Monod
   Journal: Church History 54:421-422 S 1985
    Pages: viii,411

Imprint: University Pr of America, 1984

Person as Subject: MONOD, ADOLPHE

Journals: Church History ISSN: 0009-6407

Reviewer: Nichols, James H

Keyword   : Groen van Prinsterer

ATLA RELIGION DATABASE 1996

   Year: 1994   Type: Review

   Author: Van Dyke, Harry, and Groen van Prinsterer, Guillaume, 1801-1876
    Title: Groen Van Prinsterer's Lectures on Unbelief and Revolution
   Journal: Church History 63:133-135 Mr 1994
    Pages: x,561

Imprint: Jordan Station, Ont: Wedge Pub Fndtn, 1989

Journals: Church History ISSN: 0009-6407

Reviewer: De Jong, James A

ATLA RELIGION DATABASE 1996

   Year: 1982   Type: Essay   Language: English
                                Book/Essay Link #: 82-14631

   Author: Godfrey, W Robert
    Title: Calvin and Calvinism in the Netherlands
     In: John Calvin: his influence; ed by W Stanford

Person as Subject: GROEN VAN PRINSTERER, GUILLAUME, 1801-1876
                   VOETIUS, GISBERT, 1589-1676

This is a copy of one of the printouts I would get from the UNC library on the tractor feed printers. This is a list of some of the books I found on church history and revival. I had stacks of these and would find the book, read it, take notes and mark it off the list. I still have about 40 pages from this single printout. I could go through a list of 15-20 books within two to three weeks. I was that hungry to read and would read, journal and pray. The stories taught me how to pray big prayers. I would read a story and ask GOD to do what HE did in history in our day again. This increased my faith for revival and gave me strategy in prayer and action.

In 1307's Wycliffe translated the Bible into English. He taught church reform and lost power and was persecuted because of peasant revolts

1415
John Huss was burned at the stake along with his writings. One of the greatest reformers. Saw many converted

Martin Luther
Born- 1483
had "inner experience"
in 1512

William Tyndale
Born- 1494

Menno Simons
Born 1496

1400

1500

Key

Blue- "Divine Healing involved"
Green- "Reformers"
Yellow- "Revivalist"
Pink- "person passed away"

1500

1600

1700

Feb ?, 1546
Martin Luther died

Scottish Revival
"John Welsh"
1590-1606

1536
William Tyndale died

Solomon Stoddard
Revival meetings from 1679
till 1708
"Jonathan Edward's
grandfather"

William Tennent
Born- 1673
Built the "Log College"
He influenced many during the Great
Awakening. Many converts.

Top timeline (1700–1750)

- Jonathan Edwards Born- 1703
- John Wesley Born- 1703 May 24, 1738- Aldersgate, saved
- Gilbert Tennent Born- 1703 Elder son of William Tennent w/ Frelinghuysen & traveled w/ Whitefield
- Charles Wesley Born- 1707
- George Whitefield Born- 1714 1735 England, saved & began ministry
- Francis Asbury Born- 1745 Historic Methodist circuit rider & father of American Methodism.

1st Great Awakening 1726-1776 (official beginning- 1734)
LEADERS: William Tennent (Presbyterian)
Theodore Frelinghuysen (Dutch Reformed)
Johnathan Edwards (Congregational)
Gilbert Tennent (Presbyterian)
Shubal Stearns (Baptist)
Daniel Marshall (Baptist)
Eleazar Wheelock (Founded Dartmouth, Congregational)
Henry Melchior Muhlenberg (Presbyterian)
Samuel Blair (Presbyterian)
Samuel Davies (Presbyterian)

- Howell Harris Born- 1714 Wales 1735, saved & started ministry
- 1744 Indians under David Brainerd
- 1744 (also 19) Holland- Gerardus Kuypers at Nienkirk

1700

- Zinzendorf Born- 1700 leader of the Moravians
- Shubal Stearns Born- 1706 1755 "Sandy Creek Revival" Revivalist convert of Whitefield's for the Baptists held revivals in Randolph County, NC.
- 18th cent. Welsh Revival LEADERS: Howell Harris (1714-1773) Daniel Rowland (1813-1960) William Williams (1717-1791)
- John William Tennent 1710-1723 2nd Revivals in New Jersey
- Freehold, NJ Humphrey, 1740?

1750

- 1706 William Tennent died

Bottom timeline (1750–1800)

- 1770 George Whitefield died
- Call to Prayer of 1784 Northhamptonshire, England
- Peter Cartwright Born- Sept. 1, 1785 saved with a flash of light & "Peter look to me."
- 2nd Great Awakening 1792-1870's
- 1st Great Awakening 1726-1776
- 1790 William Carey started missions

1750

- Timothy Dwight Born- 1752 (led revivals in East, 1796) J. Edwards
- 1771 Shubal Stearns died
- 1764 Gilbert Tennent died
- 1760 Zinzendorf died
- 1758 Jonathan Edwards died
- 1773 Howell Harris died
- 1788 Charles Wesley died
- Revival of the Baptists on the James River 1785 (manifestations were big, many added to their number) "May 2-6, 1990 Catch the Fire Conference"
- 1791 John Wesley died

1800

191

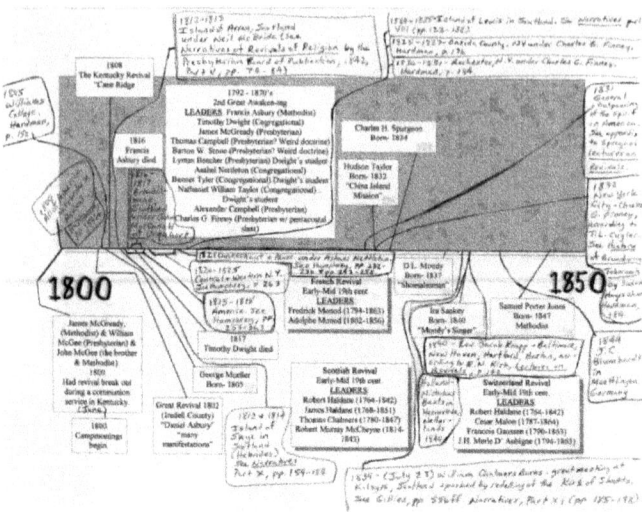

Timeline 1800–1850

1800

1850

- 1801 The Kentucky Revival 'Cane Ridge

- 1805 Williams College. *Hardman, p. 193*

- 1816 Francis Asbury died

- 1812–1813 Island of Arran, Scotland under rev'd Alex Bride (See *Narratives of Revivals of Religion by the Presbyterian Board of Publication*, 1842, Part V, pp. 76–84)

- 1792–1870's 2nd Great Awakening
  LEADERS: Francis Asbury (Methodist)
  Timothy Dwight (Congregational)
  James McGready (Presbyterian)
  Thomas Campbell (Presbyterian? Weird doctrine)
  Barton W. Stone (Presbyterian? Weird doctrine)
  Lyman Beecher (Presbyterian) Dwight's student
  Asahel Nettleton (Congregational)
  Bennet Tyler (Congregational) Dwight's student
  Nathaniel William Taylor (Congregational) – Dwight's student
  Alexander Campbell (Presbyterian)
  Charles G. Finney (Presbyterian w/ pentecostal slant)

- 1840–1825 Revival at Lewis in the Hebrides. See VIII (pp. 132–182)

- 1825–1827 Oneida County, NY under Charles G. Finney. *Hardman, p. 176*

- 1830–1831 Rochester, NY under Charles G. Finney. *Hardman, p. 194*

- Charles H. Spurgeon Born 1834

- Hudson Taylor Born 1832 "China Inland Mission"

- 1831 General Awakening at the Fall of Union NY. See appendix to Sprague's lectures on Revivals.

- 1832 New York City – Charles G. Finney, according to T.L. Cuyler. See *Hardman p. 161*

- D.H. Hill Quaker Revival 185?

- French Revival Early-Mid 19th cent.
  LEADERS
  Fredrick Monod (1794–1863)
  Adolphe Monod (1802–1856)

- 1815–1855 Opening revivals in N.Y. See Humphrey, pp 243–258

- 1825–1830 America. See Humphrey, V 263

- 1817 Timothy Dwight died

- D.L. Moody Born 1837 Shoemaker

- Ira Sankey Born 1840 "Moody's Singer"

- Samuel Porter Jones Born 1847 Methodist

- 1849 J.C. Blumhardt in Mocttlingen, Germany

- James McGready (Methodist) & William McGee (Presbyterian) & John McGee (his brother & Methodist) 1800 Had revival break out during a communion service in Kentucky. (See...)

- 1801 Camp meetings begin

- George Mueller Born 1805

- Scottish Revival Early-Mid 19th cent.
  LEADERS
  Robert Haldane (1764–1842)
  James Haldane (1768–1851)
  Thomas Chalmers (1780–1847)
  Robert Murray McCheyne (1814–1843)

- Great Revival 1802 (Iredel County) "Daniel Agnew" "many manifestations"

- 1812 & 1814 Island of Skye in Scotland (the Hebrides. The Inner Hebrides) Part X, pp. 159–158

- 1840 – Rev. Smith Riggs – Baltimore, New Haven, Hartford, Boston, acc. according to W.M. Kent, *Lectures, ...*

- Hartford Methodist Boston Worcester Phila hinds 1840

- Switzerland Revival Early-Mid 19th cent.
  LEADERS
  Robert Haldane (1764–1842)
  Cesar Malan (1787–1864)
  Francois Gaussen (1790–1863)
  J.H. Merle D' Aubigne (1794–1865)

- 1834 (July 23) in Fenwick Ayrshire during great meeting at Kilmyle, Scotland sparked by reading of the Kirk of Shotts. See Gillies, pp 586ff. *Narratives, Part X, (pp 185–192)*

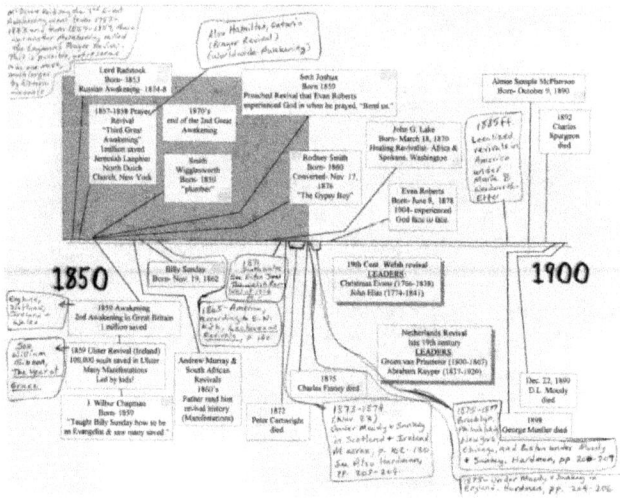

Timeline 1850–1900

1850

1900

- At Arran during the 3rd Great Awakening about 1856–1863? 1883 on I from 1859–1859 there was another Awakening in/of the Enquirer's Prayer Meetings. This is possibly another even... it was one even... which forget by Alexan records?

- Lord Radstock Born 1833 Russian Awakening 1874-8

- Alex Hamilton, Ontario's (Prayer Revival) (worldwide Awakening)

- Seth Joshua Born 1859 Preached Revival that Evan Roberts experienced God in when he prayed. "Bend us."

- Aimee Semple McPherson Born October 9, 1890

- 1892 Charles Spurgeon died

- 1857–1859 Prayer Revival "Third Great Awakening" 1 million saved Jeremiah Lanphier North Dutch Church, New York

- 1870's end of the 2nd Great Awakening

- Smith Wigglesworth Born 1859 "plumber"

- Rodney Smith Born 1860 Converted Nov 17, 1876 "The Gypsy Boy"

- John G. Lake Born March 18, 1870 Healing Revival in Africa & Spokane, Washington

- 1885ff. Localized revivals in America with/out stories in *Hardman – Ellis?*

- Evan Roberts Born June 8, 1878 1904 experienced God face to face.

- Billy Sunday Born Nov. 19, 1862

- 1859 Awakening 2nd Awakening in Great Britain 1 million saved

- 1859 Ulster Revival (Ireland) 100,000 souls saved in Ulster. Many Manifestations Led by kids!

- Andrew Murray & South African Revivals 1860's Father read him revival history (Manifestations)

- 1875 Charles Finney died

- 1872 Peter Cartwright died

- 19th Cent. Welsh revival LEADERS
  Christmas Evans (1766–1838)
  John Elias (1774–1841)

- Netherlands Revival late 19th century LEADERS
  Groen van Prinsterer (1800–1867)
  Abraham Kuyper (1837–1920)

- Dec 22, 1899 D.L. Moody died

- J. Wilbur Chapman Born 1859 "Taught Billy Sunday how to be an Evangelist & saw many saved"

- 1873–1875 under Moody + Sankey in Scotland & Scotland See Hardman, pp. 202–204

- 1875–1877 Brooklyn New York Chicago, and Boston under Moody + Sankey. *Hardman, pp 208–209*

- 1898 George Mueller died

- 1873–1875 under Moody & Sankey in England. *Hardman, pp. 204–206*

World-wide Revival

Reuben A. Torrey (1856-1928) "Congregational minister" preached during Welsh Revival

Welsh Revival Begins 1904-1905

Asbury College Revival 1905

1907 Revival Henderson, p. 213

1906 Samuel Porter Jones died

Kathryn Kuhlman Born- 1907 Ministry Began- 1923 Miracles Began- April 27, 1947

1913 Lord Radstock died

1918 J. Wilbur Chapman died

Billy Graham Born- Nov. 7th, 1918

1920? Stephen Jeffreys died

March 12, 1947 Smith Wigglesworth died

1947 Rodney Smith "the Gypsy Boy" died

Sept. 6, 1935 John G. Lake died

1944 Aimee Semple McPherson died

M'Dow + Reid another is p. 18 1934-1960

1947-1952 Mid-twentieth Century Evangelical Awakening, Billy Graham, Charles Templeton, William Branham, Gordon Lindsay, Oral Roberts, Healing & Latter Rain Revivals

1900

1908 Ira Sankey died

1908 Stephen & George Jeffreys Welsh Revivalists

1950

1905-1906 Awakening in N. America that spread throughout the U.S.

1901-1907 Charles Parham saw revivals of Pentecostal type worldwide

Azusa Street Revival (in old Methodist Church) 1906 Under William J. Seymour "Pentecostal Revival"

Los Angeles (North Bonnie Brae St., Azusa Street) Cole (Jude)

Shantung Revival Began- 1927 "Missionary revival in China."

Nov. 6, 1935 Billy Sunday died

M'Dow + Reid for Bu...: 1935-1950 p. 18 Global

Scottish Hebridean Islands Revival "Duncan Campbell" 1949 The islands were converted miraculously.

1951 Evan Roberts died

Rodney Howard Browne Born- 1968 touched- 1979 Revivals began to follow him in 1987

1962 George Jeffreys died. (He & his brother were coal miners before they entered the healing ministry!)

1967-1975 The Jesus Movement without Real People all...

December 1973 Benny Hinn touched at Kathryn Kuhlman meeting in Pittsburgh. He is forever changed.

1950

1975

1960s-1970s Charismatic Renewal (Worldwide)

1962 Beginning of Charismatic Revivals 1962- Yale Revival 1962-64- Dartmouth Revival 1962-64- Stanford Revival 1962-64- Princeton Seminary Revival

1970 Asbury Revival

193

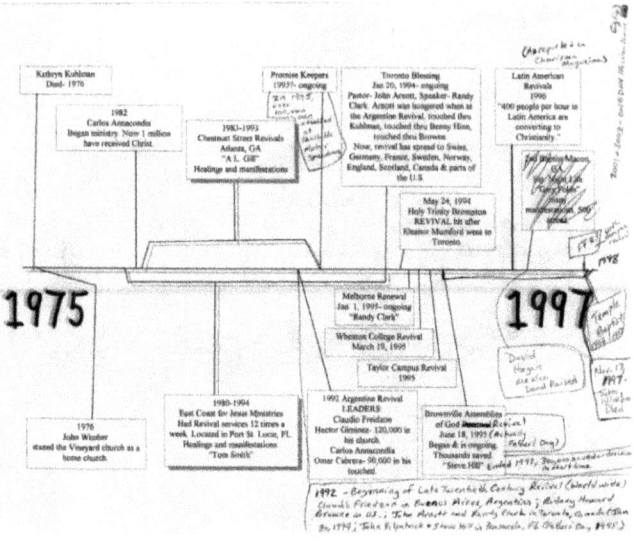

1975

1997

IMAGES FROM REVIVAL

I add these in order to just give more of a visual record from our experiences in revival. These are from Brownsville, Temple Baptist and Forest Fire as well as UNC in general to give context and background.

Almost every picture I (Dustin) took at the Toronto Airport Vineyard Christian Fellowship (as it was called back then) did not develop well. Going to that revival whether skeptical or not was a defining moment in my life. I had read about revivals and I had read John Wimber's books as well as listened to many speakers including him still did not give me comfort around seemingly weird things. My going to skeptically observe ended with a powerful encounter with GOD that left me constantly aware of HIS abiding Presence. This set me on fire and set the stage for the next years I would pray for HIM to move in power on my campus and in our church back home. This first experience with a place where GOD had come to visit and rest was the beginning of a desire to be near HIM all the time. Once you encounter GOD and feel HIM near, there is a residual hunger for   more   that   never   goes   away.

The Pensacola Outpouring which later became known as the Brownsville Revival hit the front page of many papers such as this one from one of the largest cities in North Carolina. They made the front page of prominent magazines and newspapers all over the US as well as USA Today and were on TV shows like 60 minutes. This paper was from May 28, 1997. By this time, hundreds of thousands had accepted Jesus here. I (Dustin) had been to the church many times including Spring Break of 1997 where over 14,000 college students showed up spontaneously. Beaches were empty as the church was full. It was the hottest thing around.

We all knew that being there in HIS Presence left a spiritual mark and residue. When we left, we took with us the heaviness of GOD's Presence and I truly believe that we carried this Presence with us when we were seeking GOD on campus as well as doing outreach. Every time we went, we would fill up and then leave to go back to our homes and campuses to pour out our love for HIM by sharing the Gospel everywhere HE sent us. Then we would go back for more.

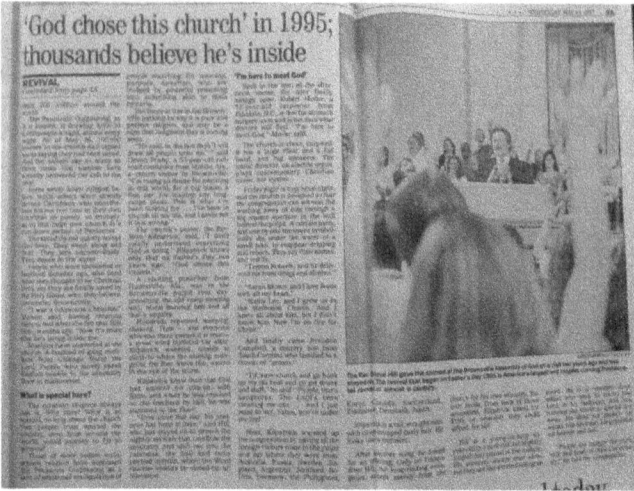

GOD truly was strong in that place. You could feel HIS Manifest Presence when you walked onto the grounds. It was heavy and real. You would et butterflies in your stomach as well as some felt twisting and just as if they wanted to bow over and not look up. It was a physical, real, awareness. I had read about revivals before 1997 and had attended Toronto, but this drove me to believe for more. Thus, the prayer closet at UNC was worth the trade of my bed and comfort.

SIGNS OF SPIRITUAL RENEWAL

Suddenly, GOD CAME

One year ago a visiting evangelist arrived in Pensacola, Florida, to conduct a Sunday service. Heaven came down, and the revival meetings haven't stopped since.

BY J. LEE GRADY

About 3:30 in the afternoon, five days a week, people begin lining up outside the front doors of Brownsville Assembly of God in Pensacola, Florida. The service doesn't

The first recording of the service from Father's Day 1995 does not show something that had "suddenly" happened. The meeting looked much more sedated than the services from the latter 1990's. This church had been praying for almost 5 years for revival on Sunday nights after their pastor had canceled the evening service to make space to pray for GOD to move in their community in revival again. Their desperation hit a climax that Sunday as Steve Hill spoke. The youth had been praying for weeks on their own for GOD to move even skipping a retreat they had all traveled to attend to stay back in their rooms and pray for revival to come. The next move of GOD may look different, but being hungry for GOD and desiring HIM more than anything else in the world is an indispensible trait of every people group I have watched in revival.

Holy Fire Ignites the Youth of BROWNSVILLE

An Interview With Richard Crisco
by Larry Walker

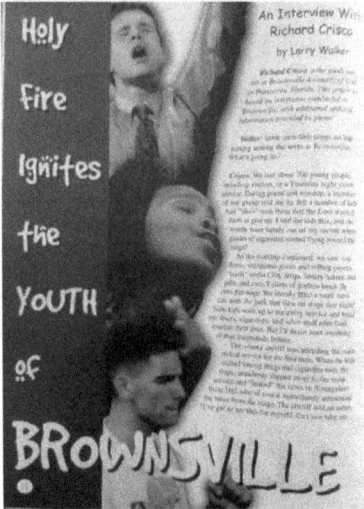

Before Forest Fire 1997 some of us got to meet and spend time with youth from the Brownsville church. Randy Greene and I spent time with them. (He helped found Chi Alpha Omega) and went on to lead movements of revival on East Carolina University that we were a part of. We became dear friends and spent a lot of time at Pensacola as well as were there during Spring Break 1997.

After Forest Fire 1997, we went down to spend time with the youth and Richard Crisco, the youth pastor. We learned so much from these young people who were also hitting the streets, sharing the Gospel with people everywhere including during a lunch break when revival broke out and school was canceled for the day because so many young people were accepting Christ, the teachers could not get them to leave the cafeteria. There were stories of how even they would run into the middle of a drug bust to tell the detained about Jesus as the police tried to make them leave the scene. These kids loved Jesus!

Many had come from abusive homes, had been addicts or even in even worse situations. When they came to Jesus, they were radically affected and changed and wanted everyone to know GOD's love.

Brownsville Assembly of GOD parking lot: This is the line to go to church. People would begin to line up as early as 3am for a 6pm entry to a 7pm nightly service. This picture was taken around 10am.

The line actually goes around the entire parking lot on the medians, turns past the furthest cars there and down the street beside the church.

The umbrellas and tents were used due to the rain. It would rain till we were drenched and no one would leave the line because they did not want to lose their space. No one cared about anything except getting inside. One night we went into the service soaked to the bone, wetter than riding water rides at a theme park and still worshiped GOD and stayed till they blinked the lights late through the night and into the next morning.

Another view from the parking lot as people are sitting on all the medians around the entire lot, weaving around until they go around the side of the building. This group is at the end of the lot. The line turns right, goes around the far side of the lot, the side of the building and down the road past the building. There were so many people along with the nearly 14,000 students that showed up that there was not enough space in even their overflow areas to seat everyone.

Brownsville Assembly of GOD from inside, "The Pensacola Outpouring." Notice all the young people in the crowd. There were 14,000 students as I stated before from all over the United States who piled into this room on the floor, on the balcony, the overflow rooms which included another sanctuary that was for the youth ministry that had around 800 seats, the choir rooms and children's ministry rooms that would hold hundreds more as well as then were seated on the front lawn outside the church in the heat to watch the services by closed circuit on a jumbo-tron screen. Many were saved, healed and delivered right there on the lawn! Many more ran down the aisle to the altar and some that did not know better, ran out of the buildings they were in and down the aisle to the main altar after crossing a street from the old building in order to get to where Steve had called them even though they did not have to. They just responded!

Me (Dustin) at Brownsville, one of the many times I went. This is literally from that Spring Break in 1997. I am a senior at UNC Chapel Hill at the time. Forest Fire 1997 had taken place earlier that February but the fire had come and we had so many invitations and more to do that I felt the need to come back for a refill. Here 20 years later in ministry, all I can say is, "WORTH IT ALL! WANTING MORE! COME QUICKLY AGAIN LORD!"

ABOUT THE AUTHOR

Dustin is a ministry veteran of over 20 years now. He has a wife,
Lori, two daughters, Anna Elizabeth and Lydia Grace and a son;
Malachi Isaac. He has traveled the globe doing ministry, missions and
church planting and is currently ministering in the DC metro area
while launching a growing software and web development firm.

Daniel has a wife and daughter and has a successful background in
business development that has included UN advisor, Microsoft
consultant out of Washington state and is currently launching a joint
venture IT and development firm with Dustin in Washington, DC.

We are the Forest Fire!

Follow us here for more information on the spread of revival in our time:

Stay in touch with us via:

Facebook: http://bit.ly/facebook-forestfire

Twitter: http://bit.ly/twitter-forestfire

Our website is here: http://theforestfire.org/

You can find many more resources there and don't forget to get our book, "The Forest Fire," on Kindle or in print!

www.ingramcontent.com/pod-product-compliance
Lightning Source LLC
Chambersburg PA
CBHW071528040426
42452CB00008B/924